Count on Math

Count on Math

activities for small hands and lively minds

By Pam Schiller
and Lynne Peterson

Illustrated by
Cheryl Kirk Noll

gryphon house®

Beltsville, Maryland

Text Illustrations: Cheryl Kirk Noll

Schiller, Pamela Byrne.
    Count on math : activities for small hands and lively minds / by
Pam Schiller and Lynne Peterson.
                            p. cm.
    Includes bibliographical references and index.
    ISBN 0-87659-188-8 (pbk.)
    1. Mathematics--Study and teaching (Elementary)   2. Mathematics—
Study and teaching--Activlty programs.   I. Peterson, Lynne, 1955-
II. Title.
QA135.5.S2825   1997
372.7'044--dc2l   97-13558
                                                         CIP

Table of Contents

Chapter 3— Classification

Chapter 4—Patterning

▥ Chapter 5—
One-to-One Correspondence

▦ Chapter 6—Ordering

Chapter 7— Numeration 1-5, Plus 0

Chapter 8—Shapes

Chapter 9— Numeration 6-10

Chapter 10— Fractions

Chapter 11— Measurement

Chapter 12— Time and Money

Introduction

Around the country, we begin workshops by asking how many people in the audience grew up liking math. Few raise their hands. When we ask why, the reasons include: "It was hard," "It never made sense" or "I had to learn it differently every year."

Most of us learned math by rote memorization and never understood the principles that form the foundation of mathematics. Children who use rote memorization to demonstrate math skills seem to advance flawlessly through the system until they reach about third grade. Then, they suddenly hit a brick wall. For the first time, the adults around them become aware that these children may not understand basic math concepts.

Children who have well developed visual memory skills can easily copy and create patterns without understanding the basic concept of patterns and how they fit into math. Children who have a well developed auditory memory can count to high numbers without understanding what those numbers represent. For all children, even those with good visual and auditory memory skills, it is important that we make sure children develop a conceptual understanding of math. The best way to achieve this goal is to present math in a developmental sequence that allows children to build on their understanding in a logical sequence and to continuously check their understanding.

This book presents a developmental approach to teaching and practicing math skills. It is grounded in the following beliefs.
1. Developmental sequence is fundamental to children's ability to build conceptual understanding.
2. Meaningful context is necessary to motivate learning.
3. Hands-on, concrete experiences give children opportunities to experiment with and to internalize new concepts.
4. Consistency in teaching ensures that rules and concepts that children learn early on will hold true through higher level math.

Developmental Sequence

Math builds on itself. Children take what they learn from one concept and apply it to the next. When they have opportunities to practice math skills in an appropriate developmental sequence, they build a solid conceptual understanding. The chapters in this book present math in a developmental sequence that provides children a natural transition from one concept to the next, preventing gaps in their understanding.

For example,

When children are allowed to explore many objects,
they begin to recognize similarities and differences of objects.

When children can determine similarities and differences,
they can classify objects.

When children can classify objects,
they can see similarities and differences well enough to recognize patterns.

When children can recognize, copy, extend and create patterns,
they can arrange sets in a one-to-one relationship.

When children can match objects one to one,
they can compare sets to determine which have more and which have less.

When children can compare sets,
they can begin to look at the "manyness" of one set and develop number concepts.

This developmental sequence provides a conceptual framework that serves as a springboard to developing higher level math skills.

Meaningful Context

Children are more motivated to learn when the material is interesting and meaningful to them. Young children operate in the here and now and are not concerned with the future. When we speak of meaningful context in this book, we are talking about math in the world of the child — counting candles on a birthday cake, sorting and classifying toys, making sure there's a one-to-one correspondence between children and cookies, and so on. The activities in this book reflect the real world of children.

Hands-on, Concrete Experiences

Young children learn by doing. When children control, manipulate and arrange objects, they internalize concepts, they make sense of the world. All activities in this book focus on hands-on, concrete experience. In every chapter, the sequence of activities is from concrete to symbolic to abstract.

Consistency in Teaching

It's important when we teach mathematics to young children that we teach rules, concepts and terminology that will always be true — from sorting and classifying to calculus. For example, using the term "set" to identify members of a group when we're classifying materials builds a concept that will be used later in numeration. Using the term "subtraction" instead of "take away" helps children learn the terminology that will hold true even when they encounter subtraction problems such as: Richele has three marbles, Tiffany has five. How many more marbles does Tiffany have than Richele?

Many of the activities in this book use small objects. If you are working with children who still put small objects in their mouths, please use caution and supervise closely.

Using This Book

This book is designed for teachers of children three through seven years old. It is organized in a developmental sequence that will take you through a full year of curriculum, no matter what age child you're teaching.

The chapters in this book and the activities within each chapter are arranged in a developmental sequence that allows children to build on what they know. Following the sequence ensures that there will be no gaps in instruction. Each chapter introduces the concept with a story, defines the concept, explains how it bridges other math concepts and provides key word vocabulary and suggestions for success.

Because of the wide gaps in ability levels between three, four, five and six year olds, each group will approach the materials in this book at a different pace. The chart below illustrates how children of different ages and in different settings may navigate the material.

50 Week Program

Concept	3's	4's	5's	6's
Free Exploration	8 weeks	6 weeks	6 weeks	3 weeks
Spatial Relationships	0 weeks	0 weeks	4 weeks	2 weeks
Classification	10 weeks	6 weeks	4 weeks	4 weeks
Patterning	12 weeks	8 weeks	4 weeks	4 weeks
One-to-One Correspondence	8 weeks	6 weeks	4 weeks	3 weeks
Ordering	4 weeks	6 weeks	4 weeks	3 weeks
Numeration 1-5		8 weeks	8 weeks	8 weeks
Shapes		4 weeks	2 weeks	2 weeks
Numeration 6-10			8 weeks	9 weeks
Fractions			2 weeks	4 weeks
Measurement			2 weeks	4 weeks
Time/Money			2 weeks	4 weeks

40 Week Program

Concept	5's	6's
Free Exploration	4 weeks	2 weeks
Spatial Relationships	2 weeks	2 weeks
Classification	4 weeks	3 week
Patterning	4 weeks	3 weeks
One-to-One Correspondence	3 weeks	2 weeks
Ordering	3 weeks	2 weeks
Numeration 1-5	6 weeks	7 weeks
Shapes	2 weeks	2 weeks
Numeration 6-10	6 weeks	8 weeks
Fractions	2 weeks	3 weeks
Measurement	2 weeks	3 weeks
Time/Money	2 weeks	3 weeks

This table is a general guide. Teachers will know best when their particular children are ready to progress to a new math concept, as well as how to integrate these concepts into their curriculum most effectively.

Each chapter ends with evaluation criteria. If the children are able to complete all aspects of that evaluation, you can assume they have a conceptual understanding of the information in that chapter and are ready to move on.

The end of a chapter does not mean the end of practice of that concept or skill. Concept development in young children is a continuous, ongoing process. All new concepts and experiences open the opportunity for expansion and often for revision of existing concepts. Once a skill or concept is introduced, it should be reviewed on a regular basis.

Activities

Activities in this book are child-centered and hands-on. They are developmentally sequenced from easiest to most difficult. Each chapter has enough activities to develop basic concepts, but feel free to customize or expand on them to meet the needs of your children.

In Chapters 1 and 2, which deal with free exploration and spatial relationships, the activities are unstructured, encouraging children to explore, experiment and make their own discoveries. The activities in Chapters 3 through 12 require more teacher/child interaction.

All chapters begin with an introductory circle time story followed by activities that allow children to gain conceptual awareness. Activities involving specific skills and concepts in each chapter are grouped under appropriate section heads.

Any Time Ideas

Any Time Ideas capitalize on teachable moments. They provide opportunities for reinforcing skills and concepts in the chapter.

Suggestions for Home Involvement

Each chapter includes a letter to families that explains what children are learning at school and provides suggestions for home support, including activities and a book list.

Observations and Evaluations

This section provides suggestions for evaluating children's progress. Children should be able to demonstrate conceptual understanding before moving on to the next chapter.

Resources

A resource section at the end of each chapter lists children's books, records and songs that support the chapter concepts. All of these provide ways to extend and integrate math concepts into other areas of the curriculum.

Enjoy *Count on Math*! We wish you and your children an exciting, fun-filled and, most importantly, a successful journey into math.

Chapter 1

Exploration of Materials

Definition

Children need an abundance of both discrete and continuous materials to explore the attributes and properties of materials. Discrete materials are those that can be counted (blocks, cookies, children); continuous materials are those that can be measured (water, sand, playdough); materials can be both discrete and continuous (gravel, cookies, children). Encourage, motivate and assist children without interfering with their exploration. The activities included in this chapter appeal to children's natural sense of curiosity.

Caution: Supervise activities closely when working with young children who still put small objects in their mouths.

Bridge to Other Math Concepts

Children need many opportunities to touch, taste, smell, listen to and visually explore a variety of materials to learn about their multiple attributes or properties. Free exploration helps children see similarities and differences in objects when they begin to practice classification.

Suggestions for Success

- ◆ Set up ground rules before you begin. Talk with the children about using and taking care of classroom materials.
- ◆ Help the children get into the habit of picking up and putting away whatever they are using before moving on to something else.
- ◆ Give children many opportunities to explore and experience the properties of a variety of materials.
- ◆ Keep a wide assortment of objects and materials available in learning centers. Rotate and change materials when the children begin to lose interest.
- ◆ Encourage the children to explore and play in each of the centers so that they experience a wide variety of activities and discoveries.
- ◆ Encourage and model frequent use of vocabulary and other descriptive words. Building vocabulary is the primary goal of this chapter.

Key Words

big/little, fast/slow	few/many	hard/soft
hot/cold	large/small	liquid/solid
rough/smooth	thick/thin	wet/dry

Circle Time Story:
The Wonderful Book of Leaves

Materials

assortment of leaves (use leaves as props as you tell the story)

One day when Austin was raking the leaves for his mom, he noticed a big red leaf in the pile. It was the reddest leaf Austin had ever seen. He stopped raking and picked up the leaf. "I'm going to keep this one," thought Austin. He put the leaf in his pocket and started to rake again.

Pretty soon, Austin had a pile of leaves ready to bag. He called to his sister Tamera to come hold the bag open. When Tamera came to help, she noticed a huge leaf right on top of the pile. "Look, Austin," she said. "This is the biggest leaf I've ever seen."

"Look at mine," Austin said, as he took the red leaf out of his pocket.

"Wow, that is neat!" said Tamera.

"I have an idea," said Austin. "Let's see how many different kinds of leaves we can find."

Austin and Tamera began to dig through the pile of leaves. They found yellow leaves, orange leaves, brown leaves and leaves that were a mixture of green and yellow. They found big leaves and small leaves; dry, stiff leaves and soft leaves. They found leaves with smooth edges and leaves with jagged edges.

"I never knew there were so many different kinds of leaves," said Tamera.

"Me either," said Austin. "Let's go show Mom."

When Austin and Tamera showed the leaves to their mother, they described each one carefully. "This one is big, yellow, soft and jagged around the edges. This one is small and brown."

After the children had described each leaf, their mother made a great suggestion. She said she thought it would be a good idea if the children made a book of leaves. Austin and Tamera were delighted.

They got paper, glue, bags and crayons and created "Austin's and Tamera's Book of Autumn Leaves."

Materials for Story Extension

six ziplock bags
six pieces of poster board cut to fit inside the bags
stapler and staples
colored tape
glue
crayons
assortment of leaves

Activity

Make a "Class Book of Autumn Leaves." Help the children stack the ziplock bags and staple them together at the bottom (the "unzippered" side). Cover the staples with plastic tape. Invite children to select a leaf and glue it on a piece of the poster board. Ask the children to describe the leaf. Transcribe their description on the poster board. Encourage the children to turn the poster board over and repeat the process. Slip the poster board inside one of the ziplock bags and zip it closed. Repeat the activity until all bags are filled.

2   Sand Table Fun

Materials

sand table or large tub of sand
strainers, funnels, scoops, buckets, spoons, bowls, nesting measuring cups

Activity

Put a variety of containers and utensils in the sand table. Encourage children to explore the characteristics of the sand using the utensils.

3   Junk Box Exploration

Materials

shoe boxes
buttons, jar lids, keys, milk jug lids, corks, spools and other interesting things

Activity

Create junk boxes for each type of material you collect. Keep all the junk boxes within easy reach for the children. Encourage children to explore the junk.

4   Playdough Squeeze

Materials

1 cup flour
1 cup water
food coloring
bowl and mixing spoon

1/2 cup salt
1 tablespoon vegetable oil
2 teaspoons cream of tartar

Activity

Invite the children to help mix flour, salt, water, oil, cream of tartar and food coloring in the bowl to make playdough. Then let the children play with it. Model rolling, pounding, stretching and squeezing, then leave the children to their own work. As the children work, ask them to describe the characteristics of the dough.

5   Textured Playdough

Materials

playdough
sawdust

sand
small pebbles

Activity

Make a large batch of playdough with the children and divide it into four portions. Mix sand in one portion, sawdust in another and small pebbles in another. Leave one portion smooth. Encourage the children to describe the different textures as they mold and play with the different portions.

6 Balancing Act

Materials

balance scale
pieces from junk boxes
playdough
manipulatives

Activity

Provide a balance scale for weighing junk materials, playdough and manipulatives.

7 Tactile Exploration

Materials

sand table or large tub of sand
packing peanuts, sawdust or gravel
assorted containers and utensils

Activity

Replace the contents of the sand table with sawdust, gravel or packing peanuts. Encourage children to explore the new material.

8 Water Play

Materials

water table
assorted containers and utensils

Activity

Set up a water table and provide strainers, colanders, basters, funnels, measuring cups and slotted and solid spoons. Encourage the children to experiment with the different utensils and water.

9   Fast or Slow

Materials

clear plastic jar of water
clear plastic jar of cooking oil
clear plastic jar of shampoo
pennies or marbles

Activity

Let children experiment with the thickness of liquids. Give them the jars of water, cooking oil and shampoo. Have them drop a penny or marble in each and watch what happens.

10   Sinkers and Floaters

Materials

water table or large tub of water
assortment of objects (feather, cotton ball, penny, paper clip, washer, straw, plastic block)

Activity

Encourage children to experiment with the objects at the water table. Which things float? Which things don't float? Ask the children to describe how the floaters are different from the sinkers.

11   Floaters and Droppers

Materials

assortment of objects (feather, cotton ball, penny, paper clip, washer, straw, plastic block)

Activity

Invite the children to experiment with the objects by tossing them in the air to see which drop and which float to the ground. Encourage children to describe the objects and the difference between the floaters and the droppers.

12   Stickers and Nonstickers

Materials

magnet
assortment of objects (feather, washer, paper clip, penny, straw, cotton ball, napkin)

Activity

Encourage the children to experiment with the objects and the magnet. Which objects stick to the magnet? Which ones don't stick? Encourage children to describe the objects and the difference between stickers and nonstickers.

13   Rock Collections

Materials

small rocks or pebbles
box

Activity

Ask the children each to select one small rock or pebble from the playground. Encourage children to discuss the color, shape and texture of their rocks. Place all the rocks into a box for further exploration.

14   Weighted Cans

Materials

coffee cans with lids
clay, sand or plaster of Paris
glue or wide plastic tape
blocks and a board to make an inclined plane

Activity

Make a set of weighted coffee cans by filling cans with different amounts of clay, plaster of Paris or sand. Seal the lids with glue or wide plastic tape. Let children experiment with rolling the cans across the floor and up and down inclined planes.

15   What Happens When . . .

Materials

plastic tub of water
three or four plastic measuring cups of varying sizes

Activity

As children play and explore, ask questions such as "What happens when you fill a large cup with water and pour it into a smaller one?" "What happens when you fill a small cup with water and pour it into a larger one?"

16   Dress Up Descriptors

Materials

scarves, hats, costume jewelry

Activity

Put scarves, hats and costume jewelry within the children's reach. Encourage exploration and recognition of such attributes as size, color, material and utility. Children may enjoy putting on a style show.

17 Feely Bag Frenzy

Materials
variety of objects (balls, blocks, puzzle pieces) in a bag

Activity
Let each child reach into the bag without looking, feel one of the objects and describe it. Encourage the child to predict what the object is, then remove it for identification.

18 Nesting

Materials
variety of nesting objects, such as plastic bowls, measuring cups and spoons, lids from jars and spray cans, boxes that fit inside each other

Activity
Put the objects in the dramatic play center for the children to explore.

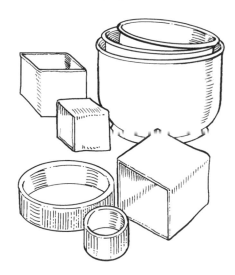

19 What Fits In?

Materials
assortment of objects and containers

Activity
Encourage the children to place individual objects in different containers. Make sure you have objects and containers in a variety of shapes and sizes. Some objects should be larger than the smaller boxes; some objects should be shaped so that they fit only in particular boxes.

20 Corkers

Materials
collection of small, medium and large corks

Activity
Invite children to create designs or build towers using the different shapes and sizes of corks.

21 Pipe Connectors

Materials
assortment of plastic pipe and connectors from hardware or plumbing supply stores cut into various lengths (use a hacksaw and sand any rough edges)

Activity
Put the pipe and an assortment of connectors in the construction center. Encourage children to explore and discuss how the pipes are different.

22 Broad Strokes

Materials
easel   paints
brushes   paper

Activity
Place both wide and narrow brushes at the easel for children to use as they paint. Ask the children to describe the different brush strokes. Try the same activity with thick and thin paints.

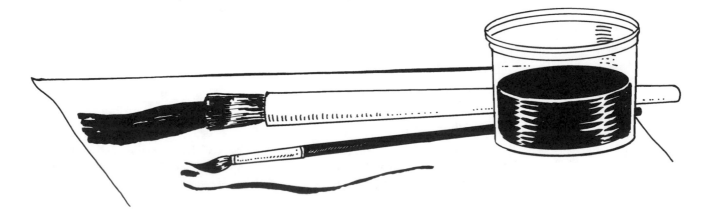

23   **What Do You Hear?**

Materials

rhythm instruments

Activity

Let children explore loud and soft sounds and high and low tones with the instruments. Ask the children to describe the sounds.

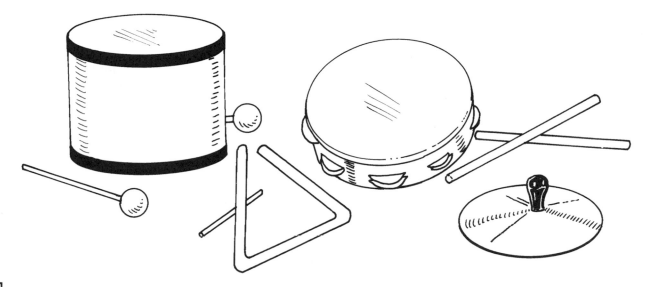

24   **Creative Structures**

Materials

cereal boxes	plastic jars with lids
shoe boxes	clean, empty milk cartons of various sizes

round canisters (potato chip and shortening containers)
papers and pens or pencils (for recording descriptions)

Activity

Put the materials in the block center for the children to use in building. Encourage the children to describe their structures. You may want to write their descriptions on sheets of paper and post them nearby.

25   **Woodworking**

Materials

variety of types and shapes of wood (ask at your local lumber yard, hardwood dealer or planing mill for free and inexpensive scraps and samples)
woodworking tools

Activity

Put wood pieces in the woodworking center. Encourage children to investigate weight, color, grain, texture and density. Make sure you have a good assortment of tools available as well.
Caution: Use caution and supervise young children closely.

26   Textured Writings

Materials

crayons   brushes
paints
variety of paper, such as heavy and light bond, newsprint, textured and card stock (You might want to make your own paper. Put 1" strips or squares of newspaper or scrap paper in a blender about 3/4 full of water and mix. Pour the mixture over a screen and let it dry. You can create an assortment of textures this way.)

Activity

Encourage children to experiment with different writing instruments (crayons, brushes, fingers, etc.) on the different papers.

27   Noise Makers

Materials

assortment of manipulatives and things from junk boxes
metal tray

Activity

Encourage the children to drop objects on the metal tray and listen to the sounds they make. What things make loud noises? What things make soft noises? What happens if you drop more than one thing at a time?

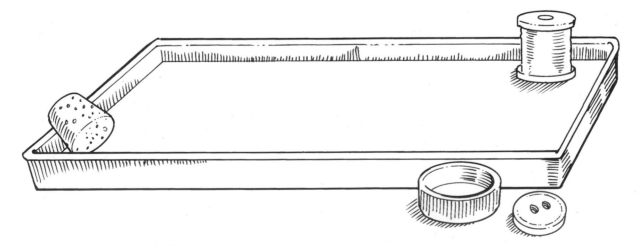

28   Gak

Materials

glue   Borax
water   bowls
spoon   measuring cups and spoons

Activity

Mix 1 cup of warm water with 2 teaspoons of Borax. In a separate bowl mix 2 cups of glue with 1-1/2 cups of water. Then, blend the two mixtures together. Let the children play with Gak. Ask them to describe it. How is it different from play-dough? Encourage the children to experiment with Gak in different temperatures (in the window, near the heating vent, near the air conditioner). Ask the children questions such as, "How does Gak change when it gets warm?"

29   Smelly Bottles

Materials

pill bottles or film canisters
cotton balls
extracts, perfumes, spices
ice pick or awl (for adult only)

Activity

Sprinkle a different extract, perfume or spice on each cotton ball. Put one cotton ball in each bottle. Punch holes in the lids. Encourage children to describe the smells.

30   Scratch and Sniff Pictures

Materials

tempera paint
strawberry, orange and lemon extracts

Activity

Mix 1/2 bottle of extract with 1 cup of tempera paint. Let the children paint. When their paintings are dry, the children can scratch and sniff them. Ask them to describe what they smell.

31 Hot and Cold Pennies

Materials

pennies

Activity

Encourage the children to put pennies in a sunny window, near an air vent, in the refrigerator, in their pocket and other warm and cool places. After a few minutes, ask children to feel the pennies and describe how they feel.

32 Shadow Watch

Materials

overhead projector

Activity

Turn on the overhead so that it shines low on the wall. Invite children to stand at different distances between the projector and the wall. How are their shadows different? How do their shadows change when they move?

33 Recipes for Fun

Materials

easy recipes (see below) and ingredients
cooking utensils

Activity

Involve children in simple cooking experiences such as making peanut butter, applesauce, gelatin or popsicles.

◆ Peanut Butter

peanuts	cooking oil
salt	crackers
blender or food processor	measuring cups and spoons

Place one cup of peanuts in a blender or food processor. Add one teaspoon of cooking oil. Blend. If the peanuts were not already salted, you may want to add 1/4 teaspoon of salt. Spread on crackers and enjoy.

◆ Applesauce

six apples

sugar

lemon juice

cutting board

stove or hot plate

measuring cups and spoons

water

cinnamon

knives

saucepan

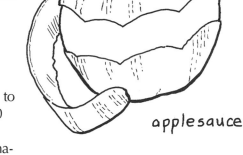

applesauce

Peel and core the apples, removing the seeds, and cut them up. Put apples and 1/2 cup of water in saucepan and bring to a boil. Reduce heat and simmer for 8-10 minutes. Add 1/3 cup of sugar, 1 teaspoon of lemon juice and a dash of cinnamon. Mix well. Cover and refrigerate until ready to serve. Makes about 3 cups of applesauce.

◆ Gelatin

gelatin mix

water

fresh fruit, optional

gelatin

Prepare your favorite gelatin mix according to the package directions. If you like, add fresh fruit (peeled, sliced, chopped). Children might also like to cut the gelatin with cookie cutters. Prepare the gelatin in a shallow pan. Chill at least 3 hours. Dip bottom of pan in warm water for a few seconds to loosen gelatin. Cut with cookie cutters, then lift out with fingers or metal spatula.

◆ Popsicles

frozen fruit juice

pitcher

small paper cups

water

spoon

popsicle sticks

Prepare the fruit juice according to directions. Pour into cups, filling them about halfway. Put in freezer. After about 30 minutes, juice will be slushy enough to hold popsicle sticks. Finish freezing.

popsicles

34   # Leaf Bracelets

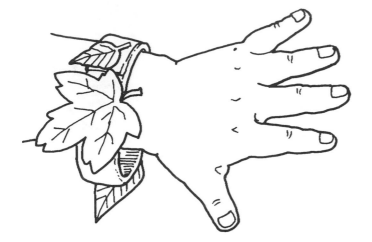

Materials

leaves
masking tape

Activity

Give children loops of masking tape (sticky side out) to wear around their wrists. Invite them on a nature walk to collect fallen leaves. Encourage children to stick leaves to their tape bracelets. Ask them to describe their bracelets to friends.

35   # Mixing Mixtures

Materials

tub of sand
bucket of water
cups, spoons or shovels

Activity

Encourage the children to experiment with different mixtures of sand and water. Ask children to discuss changes in texture and weight.

36   # Cooking Changes

Materials

Stone Soup by Marcia Brown   crockpot
clean stone   cooking utensils
beef bouillon   bowls and spoons
vegetables (ask children to bring vegetables from home)

Activity

Read *Stone Soup* to the children. Ask the children if they would like to help make their own stone soup. Put the clean stone in the pot, then invite the children to wash the vegetables they've brought. Peel and, if necessary, chop vegetables up. Talk about the attributes of each vegetable (color, size, shape, texture). Encourage children to add their vegetables to the crockpot, then cover with bouillon. Cook the soup (it will take about 2 1/2 hours). Serve the soup (perhaps the next day). As the children eat the soup, encourage them to notice and describe any changes in the color, size, shape or texture of the vegetables.

37 Crayon Melt

Materials

crayons
paper
warming tray on low
masking tape
oven mitt for non-drawing hand

Activity

Encourage children to place the paper on the warming tray and then color on the paper. (Use masking tape to hold the paper to the warming tray.) How does the heat effect the crayon? Does it change the colors? The texture?

38 Color Mixing

Materials

ice cube tray
food coloring
eyedroppers

Activity

Fill two ice cube tray sections half full with water. Add blue food coloring to one section and red to another. Give the children an eyedropper. Encourage them to mix the red and blue water in the other ice cube tray sections and describe the shades of purple they create.

39 Glue Drop Art

Materials

glue
paper

Activity

Encourage the children to squeeze drops of glue onto a sheet of paper. After the glue dries, invite children to feel the drops and describe them.

Word Web

Materials

chart paper
marker

Activity

Draw a circle in the center of the chart. Draw a picture of a cat and/or write the word CAT inside. Ask the children to tell you everything they know about cats. Write their responses around the circle. Draw lines from each word or phrase to the circle.

Any Time Ideas

◆ Take advantage of opportunities to model and encourage descriptive language.

Suggestions for Home Involvement

◆ At the beginning of school, ask parents to collect and send you empty boxes, plastic containers, corks, lids, old keys and other assorted pieces of junk. This practice serves many purposes: parents are quickly involved in their children's learning at school, children feel included and begin to take ownership of the learning process and you are able to delegate some responsibility, which can save you time.
◆ Send home a copy of Home Connections on page 36.

Observations and Evaluations

◆ Listen for children's use of vocabulary words and other descriptive words. Do children recognize and name attributes of the materials they are using?
◆ Select objects from several junk boxes. As you describe each object individually, ask children to point to and/or name the object.
◆ Ask children to describe something they cannot see. Use a feely bag or have children handle an object behind their back and tell something about it.

Resources

Children's Books

Ayres, Pam. *Guess What?* Candlewick, 1994.
Brown, Craig. *City Sounds*. Greenwillow, 1992.
Brown, Marcia. *Stone Soup*. Simon & Schuster, 1947.
Carle, Eric. *The Mixed Up Chameleon*. HarperCollins, 1984.
Carter, David. *More Bugs in Boxes*. Simon & Schuster, 1990.
Hoban, Tana. *What Is It?* Greenwillow, 1985.
___. *Is It Red? Is It Yellow? Is It Blue?* Greenwillow, 1978.
___. *Is It Rough? Is It Smooth? Is It Shiny?* Greenwillow, 1984.
Lionni, Leo. *Little Blue and Little Yellow*. Astor-Honor, 1959.
McMillan, Bruce. *Dry or Wet?* Lothrop, 1988.
Martin, Bill Jr. *Brown Bear, Brown Bear, What Do You See?* Holt, 1992.
Serfozo, Mary. *Who Said Red?* Simon & Schuster, 1988.

Records and Songs

Archambault, John and David Plummer. "I Paint Blue." *Plant a Dream*. SRA.
Moore, Thomas. "At the Easel." *I Am Special*. Thomas Moore Records.
___. "Pockets." *Songs for the Whole Day*. Thomas Moore Records.
Palmer, Hap. "This Is a Song About Colors." *Building Basic Vocabulary*.
   Educational Activities.
Scruggs, Joe. "Rock and Roll MacDonald." *Deep in the Jungle*. Shadow Play
   Records.
"Color Song" and "We're So Glad You're Here" *Where Is Thumbkin?* Kimbo.

Home Connections

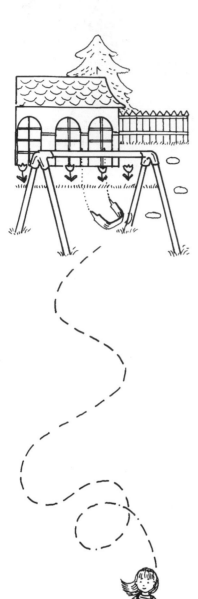

What's New? Free Exploration!

We are beginning our math program by exploring the many different materials in the classroom. As the children play and explore, they learn to recognize, identify and describe the characteristics and attributes of materials. This will help them learn to classify, make patterns and put things in order. These skills and concepts will build a foundation for learning more advanced math skills and concepts.

You Can Help

We are collecting all kinds of junk objects for the classroom — buttons, corks, lids, ribbon, cans, washers, nuts, bolts, keys, junk jewelry, etc. If you can donate any of these or similar items to our junk boxes, please send them to school with your child. Thank you!

Fun and Easy Things You Can Do at Home

◆ Let your child help you cook. Describe spices and textures.
◆ Encourage your child to start a collection of leaves, rocks or coins.
◆ Encourage your child to play with buttons, nuts and bolts, jar lids, plastic containers and other items you have around the house.
◆ **Caution**: Please use caution with young children who still put small objects in their mouths.

Vocabulary Builders

These are some of our vocabulary words. Use them at home whenever you can.
big/little
fast/slow
hard/soft
hot/cold
loud/soft
thick/thin
rough/smooth

Book Corner

Next time you visit the library, check out one of these books:
Carle, Eric. *The Mixed Up Chameleon.* HarperCollins, 1984.
Lionni, Leo. *Little Blue and Little Yellow.* Astor, 1959.
Martin, Bill Jr. *Brown Bear, Brown Bear, What Do You See?* Holt, 1992.

This page may be copied and sent home to parents.

Chapter 2

Spatial Relationships

Definition

Learning spatial relationships is beginning to understand right and left; top and bottom; the meaning of under, between, in front of, behind and other position and direction words.

Bridge to Other Math Concepts

Just as children need vocabulary that will help them describe attributes, they also need vocabulary to describe position, direction and relationships. Children will use this vocabulary and the corresponding conceptual awareness when they classify and order materials.

Suggestions for Success

◆ Take advantage of opportunities to talk about the position of people and objects.

◆ Model appropriate vocabulary. If a child uses a word incorrectly, repeat the phrase or sentence, using the correct term.

◆ Observe how children use and respond to direction and position words. Vocabulary words should be familiar and useful to children.

◆ Watch as the children draw pictures of themselves and others. Are arms and legs shown coming off the trunk? Are facial features arranged appropriately? Look for evidence of a child's understanding of spatial relationships in other drawings as well. Include representative work in the children's portfolios. Remember that it is age appropriate for young children to draw bodies and objects disproportionately. Evaluate their efforts with this in mind.

Key Words

above	around	away	back
before	behind	below	beside
bottom	center	down	end
far	finish	first	forward
from	front	here	high
in back of	in front of	inside	last
low	middle	near	next
next to	on	out	outside
over	start	there	through
top	under	up	

Circle Time Story: A Place for Pumpkin

Materials

small pumpkin
wagon, optional
(select a child to move the pumpkin to locations described in the story as the story is told)

Andre had been waiting all summer for his pumpkin to be large enough to pick. He had planted the seeds in the spring and had been watching the pumpkins grow from seeds to vines to blossoms and, finally, to small green pumpkins. He watched the pumpkins turn yellow, then orange. He watched them get bigger and bigger and bigger. Finally his daddy said, "They're ready to pick." Andre knew just which pumpkin he wanted and he knew just where he wanted to put it.

Andre walked to the **middle** of the pumpkin patch and picked his pumpkin. He put the pumpkin **in** his wagon and pulled it **through** the pumpkin patch, **over** the hill and **down** the dirt road to his house.

He took his pumpkin **out** of the wagon and went **inside** to show it to his mother. She was very surprised to see how big and round the pumpkin had grown. Andre put the pumpkin **on** the kitchen table.

"This is a perfect spot for my pumpkin," said Andre.

"Oh, no it isn't," said Andre's mother. "It's in my way."

Andre picked up his pumpkin and put it **under** the table.

"Oh, no," said Andre's dad. "That's where I put my feet."

Andre picked up his pumpkin and put it **beside** the back door.

"Oh no," said Andre's sister. "That's where I put my boots."

Andre picked up his pumpkin and put it **behind** his chair.

"Oh no," said Andre's grandmother. "That will be in your way."

Andre was discouraged. He wanted his pumpkin to be in a place where he could see it every day.

"I have an idea," said Andre's grandfather. "Let's put the pumpkin **on** the front porch, **beside** the swing, **on top of** the porch rail. Then everyone can see it!"

And so they did!

Materials for Story Extension

drawing paper
crayons

Activity

Encourage children to draw pictures of a spot where they would like to display their pumpkins. Ask them to describe their drawings.

2   Games, Games

Materials

Activity

Direct children's attention to position and direction words while playing games such as "Simon Says," "I Spy," "London Bridge," "Go In and Out the Window" and "Hokey Pokey."

3   Obstacle Course

Materials

furniture   sleeping mats
rope   masking tape
sheets   boxes

Activity

Set up an obstacle course. Have children describe their movements using appropriate terms such as over, under, through and around as they move through the course.

4 Following Directions

Materials

audio cassette recorder and tape

Activity

Record directions for a simple activity on an audio tape, emphasizing position words. Encourage children to do the activity while listening to the tape. For example, "Take some blocks from the shelf. Stack the blocks on top of each other to build a tower." You may want to create a tape for each of your learning centers.

5 Inside, Outside

Materials

plastic hoop
assortment of objects

Activity

Place a plastic hoop on the floor. Give the children a variety of small objects and ask them to place each one inside or outside the hoop.

6 Beanbag Toss

Materials

cardboard box (approximately 12" x 12")
beanbags

Activity

Invite children to take turns tossing a beanbag into a box. Ask them to describe where the beanbag lands each time (inside the box, outside the box, next to the box, behind or in front of the box, beside the box, far away from the box.)

7 Hidden Objects

Materials

familiar objects, such as books, crayons, blocks

Activity

Hide an object and give the children clues describing where it's hidden. Use as many position and direction words as possible.

8 Building Creations

Materials
blocks
empty boxes

Activity
Provide opportunities for children to build with blocks and boxes. Have them describe their creations and tell how they built them.

9 Stringing Up

Materials
long string or yarn
beads

Activity
String beads on a string hung from the ceiling. Talk about the beads going up and coming down.

10 Topsy Turvy

Materials
table
puzzles, manipulatives or materials for a favorite activity

Activity
Turn a classroom table upside down and let children work on the bottom of the table.

11   Stackable Snackables

Materials

peanut butter
graham crackers

Activity

Make sandwiches by spreading peanut butter on graham crackers. Talk about the top, middle and bottom and about other things that can be in the middle.

12   Positional I Spy

Materials

Activity

Play "I Spy" by giving clues using as many position and direction words as possible. For example, "I spy something green on top of the bookcase. I spy something square near the easel. I spy something tall on the bottom shelf."

13   Under the Table Art

Materials

drawing paper
tape
crayons and markers

Activity

Tape art paper to the underside of a table and encourage children to lie on their backs to draw. Talk about the paper under the table, the paper above their bodies, about holding the markers up and the marks on the paper.

14   Follow the Leader

Materials
none

Activity
Play "Follow the Leader." Give directions that emphasize position and direction. For example, "Go around the table. Slide down the slide. Step over the blocks." Invite the children to take turns being the leader.

15   Nesting Objects

Materials
sand or water table
sets of nesting cups, bowls and spoons

Activity
Place sets of nesting objects in the sand or water table. Encourage the children to put one nesting object inside another.

16   Home Sweet Home

Materials
dollhouse and furniture

Activity
Use a dollhouse to explore top, middle, bottom and other spatial concepts. Ask children to place the furniture in specific locations. For example, "Put the bathtub in the bathroom on the top floor. Put the table and chairs near the window in the kitchen."

Blowing Bubbles

Materials

water	dish washing liquid, such as Joy
white corn syrup	bowl
measuring cups	bubble wands and containers

Activity

Mix 2 cups dish washing liquid, 6 cups water and 3/4 cup corn syrup. Let the mixture stand in the refrigerator for four hours. Invite children to dip their bubble wands in the mixture and blow bubbles. Talk about where the bubbles go and where they land. For example, "They're going up, up, up," "They're coming down," "That one is floating out the window," "This one is falling in front of the bookshelf."

◎) 18

Left, Right

Materials

construction paper
tempera paints
flat container

Activity

Give each child a sheet of construction paper that has been folded in half. Invite children to dip their right hand in paint then make a print on the right side of the paper. Do the same with the left hand. Make a left/right bulletin board display with the prints.
Note: Children may be too young to conceptualize left and right. This activity is for vocabulary only.

19

A Closer Look Outside

Materials

Activity

Take a walk outside. Look for opportunities to use position or direction vocabulary. Ask children questions such as, "What are we walking on? What's over our heads? What's behind us? What's in front of us?"

20

Fingerplays

Materials

a book of fingerplays, optional

Activity

Say fingerplays that include position and direction words with the children. Here are two children like:

Jack-in-the-box
Jack-in-the-box (tuck thumb inside palm and close fingers around it)
Oh, so still.
Won't you please come out? (pretend to look inside closed hand)
Yes, I will! (pop thumb up)

A Little Red Apple

A little red apple hung high in a tree
I looked up at it; it looked down at me.
Come down please I cried
And that little red apple fell right on my head.

21 Nursery Rhymes

Materials

props for popular nursery rhymes, optional: use an empty toilet paper roll for Jack's candle; use a spoon, bowl and pipe-cleaner spider for Miss Muffet

Activity

Read or recite favorite nursery rhymes with the children, emphasizing position and direction words. Encourage children to act out the rhymes, using props when possible. For example:

Jack be nimble, (squat)
Jack be quick, (jump up)
Jack jump over the candlestick. (child jumps over empty toilet paper roll)

Little Miss Muffet sat on her tuffet,
Eating her curds and whey. (child sits on chair or stool and pretends to eat)
Along came a spider who sat down beside her
And frightened Miss Muffet away. (second child, holding pipe-cleaner spider, sits next to first—first child runs away)

22 Our Class

Materials

camera and film
poster board
glue or tape
marker or crayon

Activity

Take pictures of children working and playing in a variety of "spatial relationships." Invite children to help label the photographs as you mount them on the poster board. Encourage them to use position and direction words in their descriptions, such as "Mary is standing beside Dennis. Nicholas is climbing up the ladder."

JAKE IN FRONT OF KARLEIGH

MAI-LI GOING UP THE LADDER

MANUEL UNDER THE TABLE

CASSIE ON THE STOOL

EMILY IN FRONT OF DUSTY

23 Treasure Hunt

Materials
"treasure" (cookies or other snack)

Activity
Hide a "treasure" somewhere in the room. Give the children positional clues (beside, under, behind, etc.) to help them find the treasure.

24 Top, Middle, Bottom Pictures

Materials
sheets of paper
crayons

Activity
Show children how to fold a sheet of paper in three sections. Encourage them to draw a picture on the paper, using the top, middle and bottom divisions, or to draw three pictures, one using the top, another using the middle and a third using the bottom.

25 First, Next, Last

Materials
favorite storybook

Activity
Read a favorite storybook or tell a favorite story. Talk about what happens first, next and last.

26 Layered Pudding

Materials

banana pudding   vanilla wafers
bananas   utensils
individual clear plastic cups

Activity

Invite the children to help prepare the pudding and slice the bananas. Encourage them to put a vanilla wafer in the bottom of their cups, spoon in the pudding and put banana slices on top. Encourage them to talk about top, middle and bottom. Then eat the top, middle and bottom.

27 Ring Toss

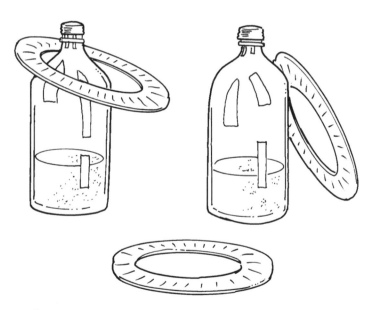

Materials

paper plates with the centers cut out
weighted cans or plastic bottles

Activity

Set weighted cans or plastic bottles a few feet from the children. Give the children the paper-plate rings and encourage them to toss the rings around the cans. Ask the children to describe where the rings land each time (around the can, leaning on the can, beside the can, etc.).

◉] 28   Drop the Clothespin

Materials

clothespins   wide-mouth jar or small box

Activity

Encourage children to stand over the jar or box and drop clothespins inside it. Ask them to describe where the clothespins land each time.

◉] 29   Pillowcase Race

Materials

pillowcases   masking tape

Activity

Mark Start and Finish lines about 10' apart on the floor. Invite children to step into a pillowcase and jump from start to finish. Talk about being inside the pillowcase, jumping up and down and moving from start to finish.

◉] 30   Back-to-Back Building

Materials

blocks or other
    construction sets

Activity

Invite two children to sit back to back. Give them identical sets of blocks. Encourage one child to build something and describe it to the other child who will then try to copy it. How similar are the two structures? How could the directions be clearer? You can also ask two children to build while you give instructions. Again, have the children sit back to back as they build. Are the two structures the same?

31　Blindfold Walk

Materials
blindfold

Activity
Invite children to work in pairs. Ask one child to wear a blindfold and the other to guide the first one around the room. Encourage the guide to hold the partner by the hand or arm and give directions (walk forward, step over the block, turn, etc.) as they walk around the classroom together. Then have the partners trade positions.

32　Candy Walk

Materials
none

Activity
Tell the children this action story about a visit to a land of candy. Encourage them to follow the directions in the story.

Have you ever been on a candy walk? It's a wonderful, sweet adventure. I'm going now. Want to come along? Okay. Stand up, close your eyes, then turn around one time. (Follow directions.) Let's open our eyes, and here we are! Wow! This looks like fun. Let's bounce up and down on the marshmallows. (Jump or bounce up and down.) Now, who wants to jump over the licorice laces? (Jump high.) Here are the candy sticks. Let's have a race to see who can climb to the top of a stick first. (Make climbing motions.) Okay. It's time to slide down. (Bend knees and squat.) Let's see who can get to the bottom first. Here's the caramel. It's sticky. Pick your feet up and put them down easily. (Move in slow motion.) Let's go behind the gingerbread house and look for candy kisses. (Move behind a shelf or wall.) Here they are! I'm going to pick some up and put them inside my pocket. (Pretend to pick up candy and put it inside your pocket.) Why don't you do the same?

Continue the story, adding directions of your own.

33　Pin the Stem on the Pumpkin (or Apple)

Materials
large cut-out pumpkin or apple
several cut-out stems
fun tack

Activity

Hang the cut-out pumpkin on the wall at children's shoulder height. Give the children cut-out stems and ask them to write their names on them. One at a time, blindfold the children, spin them around two or three times, then encourage them to stick their cut-out stem where it belongs on the pumpkin. Once they've placed their stem, remove the blindfold and ask them to describe where they put it (under the pumpkin, at the top of the pumpkin, etc.). Who put their stem in the right place?

34 Beanbag on the Pumpkin

Materials

large cut-out pumpkin
tape
three small beanbags

Activity

Tape the pumpkin to the floor. Ask children to stand about 5' away (adjust this depending on the age of your children) and toss the beanbags at the pumpkin. Who can toss all three beanbags to land on the pumpkin? Encourage children to describe where the beanbags land after each toss.

35 Twister

Materials

shower curtain with large colored circles on it (draw them with permanent markers or cut them out of contact paper)
set of index cards with a colored circle on each one (use the same colors that are on the shower curtain)

Activity

Lay the shower curtain flat on the floor. Invite children to draw a card and place either a hand or a foot on the corresponding colored circle. Continue playing (an adult or another child will have to draw the cards for them as they get tangled together). Encourage children to describe their positions and how they "fit" with the other children.

36   Mirror Talk

Materials

small hand mirrors or large
   mirror on the wall

Activity

Invite the children to look at themselves in the mirror and describe how they look. Encourage them to describe their facial features and body parts using the position words (my hair is on top of my head, my eyes are under my eyebrows, my feet are at the very bottom of me, etc.).

37   Popping Corn

Materials

markers or stickers   clean shower curtain or sheet
popcorn popper   popcorn kernels

Activity

Place the shower curtain on the floor and set the popcorn popper in the center. Fill the popper with popcorn kernels. Take the top off the popper. Invite the children to draw dots or place stickers on the spots where they think the popped corn will land when it comes out of the popper. Sit around the shower curtain, far away from the popcorn popper. Turn on the popper and check the results. Encourage the children to describe where the popcorn lands in relation to their stickers. Invite them to eat the popcorn.
Caution: Freshly popped corn is very hot. Be sure the children sit or stand far away from the popcorn popper. Wait until the corn cools before eating it.

38 Build a Room

Materials
blocks
furniture from dollhouse, optional

Activity
Encourage the children to create a model of their bedroom or other room at their home using the blocks in the block center. Ask them to describe their model.

39 Jump Frog

Materials
none

Activity
Invite the children to play Jump Frog. As they play, encourage them to describe their actions and positions ("I'm jumping over Lia." "Ben is in front of Steve." "Julio is behind Jesse.").

40 Matchbox Buttons

Materials
small matchboxes (cover the sleeve with contact paper)
buttons

Activity
Provide the children a button and a small matchbox each. Give directions for the children to place their buttons in a variety of positions. For example, "Put your button inside your box. Take your button out of the box. Place your button on top of your box."

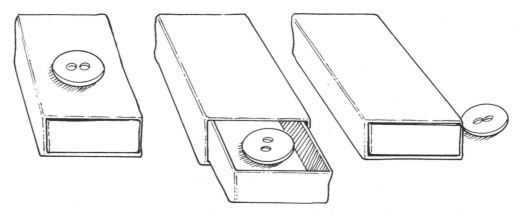

Any Time Ideas

◆ Ask children to tell where they stand in relation to other children when lining up. For example, "Leah is first. Jill is behind Tamera and in front of Mike. John is last."

◆ During the day, ask children to tell where they are in relation to other children or objects in the room. For example, "... beside Richele ... in front of the library ... in the block center."

◆ As children take out and put away materials, encourage them to use position words to tell about what they are doing (taking the crayons out of the bucket, putting the blocks inside the bucket, etc.).

Suggestions for Home Involvement

◆ Encourage children to work with their families to create a simple map showing the route they take from home to school.

◆ Send home a copy of Home Connections on page 56.

Observations and Evaluations

◆ Show children two objects, such as a crayon and a book. Place the objects in a variety of positions, each time asking children to describe the position of each object. If children cannot accomplish this, repeat Activities 4-10, 13, 15 and 39-40.

◆ Give children a small block and a coffee can. Ask them to place the block in specific positions relative to the can (inside the can, under the can, next to the can). If children cannot accomplish this, repeat Activities 4-10, 13, 15 and 40.

◆ Ask children to describe the position of things they cannot see at the time, such as the spot they're dropped off and picked up from at school (in front of the school, by the cafeteria) or the swing set (outside, behind the school). If children cannot accomplish this, repeat Activities 30, 31 and 38.

Resources

Children's Books

Allen, Jonathan. *Up the Steps, Down the Slide*. Morrow, 1992.

Berenstain, Stan and Jan Berenstain. *Inside, Outside, Upside Down*. Random House, 1968.

Brett, Jan. *The Mitten*. Putnam, 1990.

Hartman, Gail. *As the Crow Flies: A First Book of Maps*. Simon & Schuster, 1991.

Hoban, Tana. *Over, Under, and Through and Other Spatial Concepts*. Macmillan, 1973.

Hutchins, Pat. *Rosie's Walk*. Simon & Schuster, 1968.

Matthias, Catherine. *Over-Under*. Children's, 1984.

Records and Songs

Beall, Pamela Conn and Susan Hagen Nipp. "I'm a Little Teapot." *Wee Sing Children's Songs and Fingerplays*. Price Stern Sloan.

___. "The Green Grass Grows All Around." *Wee Sing Silly Songs*. Price Stern Sloan.

Little Richard. "Itsy Bitsy Spider." *For the Children*. Disney.

Millang, Steve and Greg Scelsa. "Hokey Pokey." *Kidding Around with Greg and Steve*. Youngheart.

___. "Loop D Loo." *We All Live Together, Volume 1*. Youngheart.

Mr. Al. "Rock 'N Roll Body Parts." *Mr. Al Sings and Moves*. Melody House.

Scruggs, Joe. "Put Your Thumb in the Air." *Deep in the Jungle*. Shadow Play.

"Open, Shut Them," "The Grand Old Duke of York," and "Do Your Ears Hang Low?" *Where Is Thumbkin?* Kimbo.

Home Connections

What's New? Spatial Relationships!

The children are exploring spatial relationships. Understanding spatial relationships will help children develop an understanding of direction and position such as behind, under, in front of, next to and so on.

Just as children need vocabulary to describe attributes, they also need vocabulary to describe position, direction and relationships. Children will use this vocabulary and the corresponding conceptual awareness when they classify and order materials.

Fun and Easy Things You Can Do at Home

◆ Go on walks together. Look at how things like playgrounds and buildings are put together.
◆ Gather empty boxes and canisters and build with your child.
◆ Encourage your child to help put away groceries and toys or rearrange the furniture.

Vocabulary Builders

These are some of our vocabulary words. Use them at home whenever you can.

behind	beside
in	near
on	out
top/middle/bottom	under

Book Corner

Next time you visit the library, check out one of these books:

Berenstain, Stan and Jan Berenstain. *Inside, Outside, Upside Down*. Random House, 1968.

Hoban, Tana. *Over, Under, and Through and Other Spatial Concepts*. Simon & Schuster, 1973.

Hutchins, Pat. *Rosie's Walk*. Simon & Schuster, 1968.

This page may be copied and sent home to parents.

Chapter 3

Classification

Definition

Classification is sorting and grouping objects based on the similarities and differences of the attributes of those objects.

Bridge to Other Math Concepts

When children know the vocabulary and understand the concepts of attributes (chapter 1) and spatial relationships (chapter 2), they are ready to take what they know about similarities and differences and sort and classify materials. Children will need plenty of practice grouping and regrouping materials. This will occur naturally as they become aware of multiple attributes. Children will need to understand similarities and differences to create patterns and make set comparisons.

Suggestions for Success

◆ Allow children to develop their own criteria for sorting.
◆ Use structured activities with specified criteria to encourage children to experiment and look at materials in different ways. The ability to see and use materials and ideas in more than one way is crucial to problem solving and to creative thinking and doing.
◆ As the children work with the materials, ask them to describe their criteria for classification. Restate their descriptions to include and model appropriate mathematical language. For example, "This set is made up of red blocks."
◆ Note: Children may use geometric shapes to form sets. At this point, children are using visual recognition and not a true understanding of the shapes' attributes (number of corners and sides). Shapes and their attributes will be taught after numeration when children have a conceptual understanding of "manyness." For example, children must understand what three is before they are able to make sense of three sides and three corners of a triangle.

Key Words

alike	classify	color
different	group	member
not	regroup	same
set	shape	size
sort		

Circle Time Story:
Tracie Turkey

Materials

flannel board cutouts of a turkey, pig, horse, cat, dog, duck, cow, bird and mouse, or use drawings on page 253 (use as animals are mentioned in the story)

Tracie Turkey hatched from her egg one cool Spring morning. She opened her eyes, shook from the cold and immediately began to look for her parents. She looked up. She looked down. She looked to both sides. She saw not one living thing.

"Hmm," thought Tracie. "I wonder who I belong to."

Tracie decided to take a look around. She walked out of the barn and into the barnyard. She saw two pigs.

"Hi," said Tracie. "Do I belong to you?"

"Well, let's take a look," grunted the pigs. "We have a snout and a curly tail, do you?"

"No, I don't think so," said Tracie.

"Then you don't belong to us," said the pigs.

Tracie said goodbye to the pigs and continued her search.

Soon she saw a pair of horses. "Good morning," said Tracie. "Do I belong to you?"

"No," neighed the horses. "We have long, flowing tails and lovely manes. You don't look anything like us."

"You're right," said Tracie. "Thank you for your help. I'll look behind the barn." And off she went.

Behind the barn, Tracie saw two cats drinking from a saucer of milk. "Hi," said Tracie. "Do I belong to you?"

The cats started to laugh. "Do you have fur, four legs, pointed ears and a long, skinny tail?"

Tracie started to laugh. "I don't think so," she said.

The cats suggested Tracie go to the pond and look at her reflection so she would know what she looked like. So she did. She saw feathers, a long neck, two skinny legs and a red beak.

Tracie turned around and looked across the barnyard. She saw ducks, dogs, horses, cows, pigs and cats. She saw birds and field mice and . . . what's that? They have feathers, long necks, skinny legs and red beaks. Tracie ran to the turkeys.

"Do I belong to you?" she asked.

"Oh, yes," said the turkeys. "And we are so glad you're here!"

"Me, too," said Tracie. And she smiled a big turkey smile.

Materials for Story Extension

tempera paint
shallow pan
drawing paper
crayons

Activity

Pour tempera paint into the shallow pan. Invite children to place a hand in the paint, then

make a handprint on their paper to create a turkey. Encourage children to add features, such as eyes, gobbler and legs. Ask children to describe their turkeys and to tell you one way a turkey is different from a dog. Write their answers on the paper.

2   Classify Children

Materials

Activity

Arrange the children in sets according to eye color, hair color and other criteria. After demonstrating and explaining several groupings, create another and ask the children to identify your criteria. Encourage the children to think of any criteria that would allow Tracie Turkey to be part of a group.

3

All Mixed Up

Materials

buttons, spools, bottle lids
three containers

Activity

Mix all the materials into one pile. Have the children sort them into three containers. Evaluate the results by asking the children to state the criteria they established. Are there other ways the materials could be grouped?

 4

Classroom Organization

Materials

variety of materials

Activity

Discuss how materials (books, blocks, etc.) in the room are classified and grouped.

 5

Organizing Learning Centers

Materials

learning center materials

Activity

Invite children to help sort and classify materials in learning centers. Is there more than one way to classify the materials?

6

Nature Sort

Materials

natural objects
several boxes or other containers

Activity

Encourage children to gather a few fallen leaves, twigs and stones from the playground. Provide a box for each type of item and have children sort their materials into the boxes.

 7 **Junk Box Sorting**

Materials

junk boxes

Activity

Empty all the things collected for free exploration into one big pile. Let the children sort the junk. Ask them to describe the results.

 8 **Sorting Solutions**

Materials

bag or bucket   sand, rocks, birdseed
colander   strainer
three empty containers

Activity

Mix sand, rocks and birdseed in a bag or bucket. Let the children use the colander and strainer to sift and separate the mixture into the containers. Have the children describe both the process they used and the results.

9   # Group, Regroup

Materials

dress-up clothes

Activity

Place all the clothes on the floor. Ask the children to help you sort the items into two or three groups. Encourage children to find other ways to sort the same items (hats, dresses, shoes; men's clothing, women's clothing, children's clothing; or red clothes, blue clothes, yellow clothes).

 10   # Art Sort

Materials

tempera paints and paintbrushes	markers
crayons	drawing paper

Activity

Provide tempera paints, markers and crayons in the art center. Encourage children to create a picture using one of the mediums. Later on in the day help the children sort the pictures according to the medium used. Place them on the floor to create a graph. Which medium was used most often?

 11   # Floaters, Droppers and Sinkers

Materials

assortment of objects (feather, cork, button, washer, sponge, penny, packing peanut, etc.)
water table
chart paper and marker

Activity

Make a chart with two columns, Does and Does Not. Encourage children to explore materials first to see which float and which drop when tossed into the air. Then explore materials in the water to determine those that sink and those that float. Do any of those that float in the air also float in the water?

12 # Translucent Materials

Materials

assortment of objects (paper, block, fabric scraps, cardboard, plastic, sandpaper, etc.)
flashlight

Activity

Encourage children to test each item to determine whether the light from the flashlight will shine through it. Have them make two groups of materials—translucent (light shines through) and not translucent (light does not shine through).

 13 # Land, Sea and Air

Materials

plastic animals, including birds, mammals, reptiles, amphibians and fish

Activity

Invite children to sort the animals by where they live.

 14 # Magnet Sort

Materials

assortment of objects (penny, button, feather, crayon, washer, paper clip, toy car, etc.)
magnet

Activity

Ask children to explore materials to determine which items can be picked up with a magnet and which cannot.

15 ## Ball Sort

Materials

an assortment of balls (tennis, baseball, Ping Pong, basketball, soccer, golf, etc.)

Activity

Encourage the children to sort the balls according to use. Ask them to sort again, this time according to size.

 CLASSIFYING OBJECTS BY COLOR

ACTIVITES **16** TO **25**

 16 ## The Eyes Speak

Materials

Activity

Encourage the children to group themselves according to eye color. Then try the same activity using hair color. Which children were in the same group both times?

 17 ## Colored Squares

Materials

2″ squares cut from four colors of construction paper

Activity

Provide colored squares for the children to look at. Encourage them to describe how the squares are alike and how they are different. After children have determined that the squares differ by color, have them sort the squares accordingly.

 18 ## Classroom Colors

Materials

chart paper and marker

Activity

Invite children to look around the classroom for materials they can classify by color (crayons, jackets, manipulatives, paints, etc.). Make a list on the chart paper.

19 My Favorite Color

Materials

4" squares cut from primary colored construction paper
butcher paper
glue

Activity

Allow each child to choose a
favorite color square. Invite children to form a human graph by
lining up according to the color
they chose. Which line is longest?
Encourage children to make
another graph by gluing their
squares on a big piece of butcher paper. Post the graph on the
bulletin board. Will anyone
change their color choice by the
end of the week?

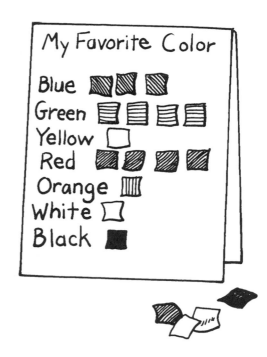

20 Color Cups

Materials

crayons
cups

Activity

Have the children sort crayons from the art center into cups according to color.

21 Color Mystery

Materials

vanilla pudding divided into three bowls; mix red food coloring in one bowl of pudding, blue in another, leave the third bowl plain
spoons, one for each child

Activity

Invite the children to taste each color of pudding and select the one they like best.
Graph the results. Ask children if they selected their choice because of taste or
color. Tell them your secret.

22   Fall Leaf Sort

Materials

fall leaves
wax paper and iron, optional

Activity

Encourage children to classify the leaves according to color. The leaves can be grouped then pressed between two sheets of wax paper.

23   Rainbow Mosaic

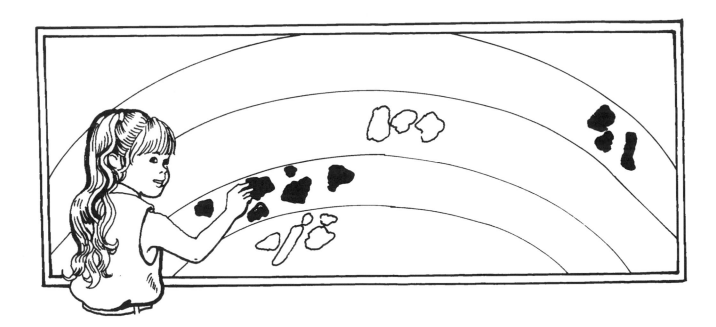

Materials

scrap pieces of red, blue, yellow and green construction paper
6' length of bulletin board paper with a four-tier rainbow drawn on it
glue

Activity

Have children tear the construction paper into any shapes they wish and then glue them on the appropriate tier of the rainbow. You will need to designate which color will go in each tier. Ask children for their suggestions.

24 Streamer Dance

Materials

2' streamers cut from red, blue, yellow and green crepe paper
red, blue, yellow and green plastic tape cut into 10' strips and placed on the floor
music

Activity

Play music and encourage the children to dance with their streamers. When the music stops, have the children move to the tape line that is the same color as their streamer. Start the music and let children mingle again. Next time the music stops, let children exchange streamers with a friend. Repeat the activity.

25 Clothespin Drop

Materials

3 one-pound coffee cans covered in red, yellow and blue construction paper
clothespins either painted or taped with plastic tape to match the cans

Activity

Play "Drop the Clothespin" matching clothespins to colored cans.

 CLASSIFYING OBJECTS BY SIZE

ACTIVITES 26 TO 35

26 Big and Little

Materials

one large box
one small box
small and large materials, such as books, pencils, crayons, cars, etc.

Activity

Encourage children to sort the materials by placing big items in the big box and small items in the small box. Are there items that will fit in both boxes? Invite children to look around the room for other items they can place in the big and little boxes.

27 Clothing Sort

Materials

sets of clothing items distinctly different in size (child's shirt, adult's shirt; child's sock, adult's sock, etc.)

Activity

Encourage children to separate the items into two stacks, large and small.

28 Three Bears Sort

Materials

"The Three Bears" (any version)
three stuffed bears to represent characters
flannel board
drawings on page 256

Activity

Make flannel board cutouts using the drawings on page 256. Arrange the cutouts on the flannel board as you read or tell the story. When you are finished, discuss the different size of the objects in the book. Let the children find items in the classroom that might belong to each bear.

29 Playdough Ball Sort

Materials

playdough
two plastic bowls, one with a large circle drawn in the bottom and one with a small circle drawn in it

Activity

Have children roll playdough into large and small balls and place them in the bowls according to size.

30 # Big and Little Animals

Materials

plastic animals or pictures of animals

Activity

Encourage children to sort the animals according to size. Ask them to explain how they determined which animals went into each category.

  31 # Building Size Vocabulary

Materials

chart paper or butcher paper and marker

Activity

Ask children to describe the size of an object in the room, using big or little as part of their description. Ask them to think of words that mean the same as big and little. Make a word chart for each.

  32 # Does It Fit?

Materials

pairs of shoes of different sizes

Activity

Place shoes in the dramatic play center and let children classify them into categories of too big, too little, just right.

33   **Name Sort**

Materials

sentence strips
marker
scissors

Activity

Print one child's
name on each
sentence strip.
Cut the strips to
size. Encourage
children to sort
the strips by long
and short names. Have them explain how they decided which names
went into each group.

34   **Big and Little Pictures**

Materials

large and small pieces of drawing paper
crayons or markers

Activity

Give each child a large and a small piece of drawing paper. Invite the children to
draw a picture on each piece of paper. When they are finished, display their work
on the bulletin board in two areas marked "Big" and "Little."

35   **Big Group, Little Groups**

Materials

yarn   scissors
marker   index cards

Activity

Create two circles, one big and one little, with the yarn. Invite the children to brainstorm a list of activities that take place throughout the day. List big group activities
on index cards and place them in the big circle. List small group or individual activities on index cards and place them in the little circle.

36 # Familiar Shapes

Materials

familiar shapes (hearts, flowers, circles) cut from one color of construction paper

Activity

Place the shapes on the floor. Let the children discuss how the shapes are alike and different. When the children have determined that the cutouts differ in shape, encourage them to classify the shapes accordingly.

 37 # Classroom Shapes

Materials

Activity

Point to the clock. Ask the children to find other items in the classroom that are round. Point to a book and ask the children to name other items that are the same shape. Invite the children to continue playing.

 38 # Art Shapes

Materials

paper cut into shapes (circle, square, triangle)
paints

Activity

Encourage children to pick a shape and make a painting on it. When the paintings are dry, have children put them on the bulletin board with other paintings of the same shape.

39 ## Cracker Snackers

Materials

assortment of shaped
   crackers
napkins

Activity

Serve each child an
assortment of crackers
for snack. Invite children
to sort their crackers
before they eat them.

40 ## Cookie Shapes

Materials

playdough
cookie cutters

Activity

Give the children cookie cutters and playdough and have them make "cookies."
Encourage the children to classify their "cookies" according to shape.

41 ## Stackable Snackables

Materials

bread and cheese cut in a variety of shapes

Activity

Encourage children to select two pieces of bread and one piece of cheese, all the
same shape, to build a sandwich for snack.

42

My Favorite Shape

Materials

9" x 12" poster board
construction paper cutouts
 (cut one square, circle, rectangle, triangle, oval and
  diamond from each color—
  red, orange, yellow, green,
  blue and purple)

Activity

Make a shape chart on the
poster board. Draw lines to
create six rows across the
paper. Put a different shape on
each line. Demonstrate placing
the matching shapes on the
appropriate lines, then invite
the children to continue the
chart.

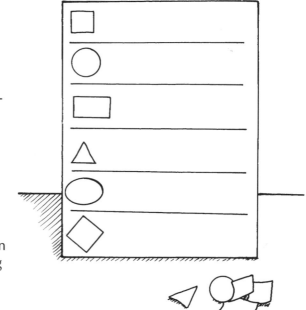

 43

Block Structures

Materials

blocks

Activity

Invite children to sort the blocks according to shape. Encourage them to build a
structure in the block center using only one shape of block.

 44

Shape Dancing

Materials

construction paper cutouts of circles, squares and triangles
outline large shapes on the floor with masking tape
music

Activity

Give the children shape cutouts and ask them to find the corresponding shape on
the floor. Play the music and have children march around the outlines. When the
music stops, the children can exchange cutouts and repeat the activity. Encourage
children to look at the groups they form.

45 # Shape Rubbings

Materials

cardboard cutouts of circles, squares and triangles
crayons
drawing paper

Activity

Have children create a design on their paper with rubbings of one shape. Remind them to change paper when they change shapes.

 CLASSIFYING OBJECTS USING OTHER SENSES

ACTIVITIES **46** TO **50**

 46 # Sweet, Not Sweet

Materials

sugar	raisins	pretzels
marshmallows	popcorn	saltine crackers

Activity

Set up a snack table with items listed above. Talk about sweet and not sweet. Let the children taste the sugar to establish their concept of sweet. Ask children to taste the other foods on the table to determine which are sweet and which are not sweet. Have them sort the items as sweet or not sweet.

47 Soft, Not Soft

Materials
fabric scraps

Activity
Provide a variety of fabric samples and encourage children to classify them as soft and not soft.

48 Pleasant, Not Pleasant

Materials
cotton balls
different extracts, perfumes, spices

Activity
Dampen the cotton balls with the extracts, perfumes and spices. Have the children classify the scents as pleasant and not pleasant.

49 Noises Inside and Outside

Materials
none

Activity
Name a noise (telephone ringing, doorbell, car motor, rain falling, etc.) and have the children determine whether they hear it inside or outside. Can they hear any of the noises inside and outside?

50 Feely Shapes

Materials
pairs of items
pillowcase

Activity
Place an assortment of paired items in the pillowcase. Ask a child to put both hands in the pillowcase and find two items that are the same, using only the sense of touch.

51 **Button #4**

Materials
buttons

Activity
Create a set of four buttons. Three of the buttons should have like attributes and the other should be different. See if the children can determine which button does not belong with the others.

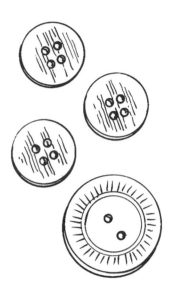

 52 **Hide a Button**

Materials
buttons

Activity
Hide a button. Show the children two other buttons, one of which is exactly like the hidden one. Give clues that describe the hidden button until the children are able to determine which of the two buttons is like the hidden one. Show children the hidden button so they can check their choice.

 53 **The Lost Button**

Materials
Frog and Toad Are Friends by Arnold Lobel
buttons

Activity
Read "The Lost Button" from the book. Provide a container of buttons for the children to classify according to size, shape, color, number of holes and thickness.

Overlapping Categories

Materials

three pieces of yarn 3' long
marker

three pieces of paper
buttons

Activity

Use the pieces of yarn to make three circles on the floor. On each of three pieces of paper, write the name of a different attribute describing a button. Place one paper upside down in each circle. Have each child select a button. One at a time, have the children place their button in one of the circles until you tell them that their button matches the (hidden) description. Continue until all the buttons have been placed or the children have guessed what is written on the papers inside the circles.

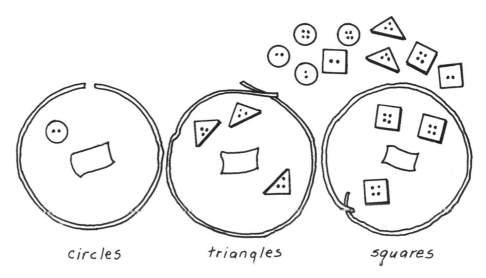

circles   triangles   squares

After children are familiar with the circle game, make the game more challenging by overlapping the circles.

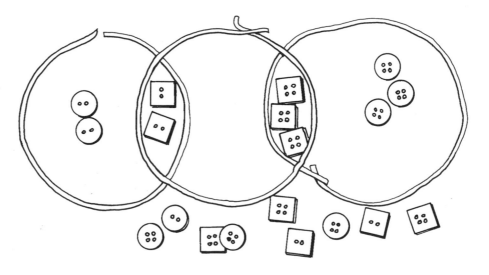

55 ## Button, Button

Materials

six-section egg carton
buttons
glue

Activity

Glue a different button in the bottom of each section of the egg carton. Place the egg carton with the button canister. Encourage the children to determine the criteria to use in placing like buttons in each compartment.

 56 # Laundry Sort

Materials

laundry basket, optional, and clothes, towels, blankets and other "laundry" from
    dramatic play center

Activity

Encourage children to sort the laundry in a variety of ways (things we wear/things we don't wear; things we wear on different parts of our body, etc.) How many ways can the children think of to sort the items?

 57 # Leaf Sort

Materials

variety of leaves
large sheet of butcher paper or shower curtain
marker

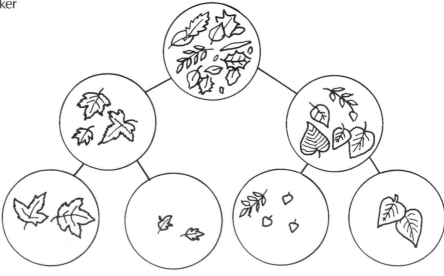

Activity

Draw circles (approximately 8" in diameter) on the butcher paper as shown. Place all the leaves in the top circle. Invite children to classify the leaves into two sub-groups, then from each subgroup into two more subgroups. Try doing this activity with other objects (buttons, keys, jar and bottle lids, etc.).

58   Shoe Sort

Materials

children's shoes

Activity

At circle time, have children take off their shoes and place them in the middle of the circle. Ask if they can think of a way to sort the shoes. After they've placed the shoes into categories, ask the children to think of another way they could sort the shoes.

59   Feeling Faces

Materials

patterns on page 255   scissors
markers   laminate or clear contact paper

Activity

Make several copies of the drawings on page 255. Color each expression a different color, cut the faces out and laminate them. Encourage children to sort the faces in different ways (color, feeling, size).

60   Birds of a Feather

Materials

Activity

Ask children a simple yes/no question that relates to opinions or preferences. For example, "Do you like broccoli? Do you like blue?" Ask all children who answer "yes" to stand in one area of the room. Ask those who answer "no" to stand in another area. Continue with a series of questions, asking the children to move across the room according to their answers. Encourage children to notice the groups they form. Add multiple choice questions ("Would you rather play soccer or read a book?"), assigning areas for children to stand. Lead the children to under-stand that people can be classified according to what we think and do.

61

Sorting Secrets

Materials

thread or yarn
buttons

Activity

Encourage children to string buttons that match their choice of attributes and then let their friends guess their sorting secret.

 62

Everyday Objects

Materials

several small bags
with five small
objects in each

Activity

Encourage children to classify the items in the bags according to their own criteria. Model the language, "Things that are and things that are not." For example, a child might place a button, a plastic spoon and a plastic lid into one pile and the remaining items, a penny and a paper clip, in another pile. The criteria would be "Things that are plastic and things that are not."

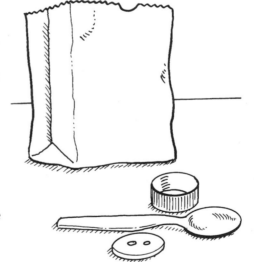

63 Classifying Friends

Materials

Activity

Ask a group of children to stand. Invite their classmates to determine ways to classify them into two groups.
Note: Be sensitive to classifications that may be hurtful to some children.

64 Group Sorting

Materials

Activity

Invite four children to select one object each from the room to create a set of objects for the whole class to sort.

65 Sorting My Way

Materials

variety of small objects

Activity

Provide a variety of small objects with overlapping classifying criteria (color, shape, size, utility, etc.). Encourage children to sort the objects into sets using any criteria they wish.

 ILLUSTRATING REAL-LIFE APPLICATIONS OF CLASSIFICATION

ACTIVITIES 66 TO 70

66 Classification at Work

Materials

paper and markers

Activity

Take a tour of the school. Visit other classrooms, the administration office, the library and the kitchen. Ask the workers to tell how they use classification in their jobs. When children return to the classroom, have them dictate an experience story about what they learned on the tour of their school.

 67 **Reclassifying the Classroom**

Materials

Activity

Help the children remember their experiences from Activities 4 and 5 of how objects and materials in the classroom are classified and organized. Is there any other way the classroom could be organized? Try some of the children's ideas. What works and what doesn't?

 68 **Puzzle Organizers**

 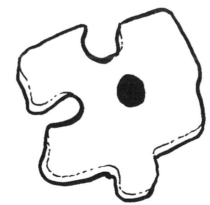 

Materials

four puzzles
markers or round colored stickers

Activity

Get four puzzles of a like size and material (wood, cardboard, etc.). Mark the back of each puzzle with a different color marker. Mix the pieces from all four puzzles together, then have the children sort them by color before putting them together.

69   ## Classification at Home

Materials

Activity

Discuss ways we classify and organize things in our homes. Talk about ways we can classify clothes. Let the children identify ways to classify their toys.

70   ## Field Trip

Materials

Activity

Take a field trip to a zoo, grocery store or post office. Encourage children to notice how things are classified.

Any Time Ideas

◆ Place a different colored sheet of construction paper in each center. Make center assignments by letting children draw corresponding color tiles from a bag or box.
◆ Classify the children according to how they travel from home to school.
◆ Talk about classification when putting away the classroom materials. How are materials grouped? Do all the blocks go together? Does size make a difference in how things go together? Are teacher's and children's supplies separated or stored together?
◆ Send children to learning centers by asking for those fitting certain criteria, such as those wearing tennis shoes or those whose name starts with the letter M.

Suggestions for Home Involvement

◆ Ask children to bring a toy from home. Put all the toys together in the center of the circle and encourage the children to sort them into categories.
◆ Send home a copy of Home Connections on page 85.

Observations and Evaluations

◆ Ask children to compare two objects and determine whether they are alike or different. Ask the children to explain how they made their decisions. If children cannot accomplish this, repeat Activities 3, 6-8, 11-12 and 48-49.

◆ Give children an assortment of junk box materials and ask them to sort the junk into sets. When children are finished, ask for explanations. If children cannot accomplish this, repeat Activities 3, 6-8, 30, 39, 56-57 and 64-65.

◆ Show two similar objects, such as two straws. Ask children to tell you how the objects are alike (they're long and skinny, there's a hole through the middle, we can drink through them) and how they are different (this one's paper, this one's plastic; this one bends, this one doesn't; this one has a red stripe on it, this one doesn't). If children cannot accomplish this, repeat Activities 57-58 and 63.

Resources

Children's Books

Accorsi, William. *Billy's Button*. Greenwillow, 1992.
Gammell, Stephen. *Once upon MacDonald's Farm*. Simon & Schuster, 1990.
Hoban, Tana. *Is It Red? Is It Yellow? Is It Blue?* Greenwillow, 1987.
___. *Is It Rough? Is It Smooth? Is It Shiny?* Greenwillow, 1984.
Lionni, Leo. *Little Blue and Little Yellow*. Astor-Honor, 1959.
Lobel, Arnold. "The Lost Button" from *Frog and Toad Are Friends*. HarperCollins, 1970.
Pluckrose, Henry. *Sorting*. Children's Press, 1995.
Sis, Peter. *Beach Ball*. Greenwillow, 1990.

Records and Songs

Archambault, John and David Plummer. "I Paint Blue." *Plant a Dream*. SRA.
"Monster and Color Game." *Monsters and Monstrous Things*. Kimbo.
Moore, Thomas. "At the Easel." *I Am Special*. Thomas Moore Records.
Palmer, Hap. "This Is a Song About Colors." *Building Basic Vocabulary*. Educational Activities.
"Color Song." *Where Is Thumbkin?* Kimbo.

Home Connections

What's New? Classification!

Your child will be learning to sort objects by their similarities and differences. This will help in understanding later math concepts like odd and even numbers and begin the foundation for advanced concepts such as numbers divisible by five, positive and negative integers and much more.

Fun and Easy Things You Can Do at Home

◆ Encourage your child to help you put away the groceries.
◆ Let your child help fold the clothes and sort them according to where they go or who wears them.
◆ Give your child jar lids, buttons, corks, other small objects and containers for sorting.
◆ Let your child put away the silverware.

Vocabulary Builders

These are some of our vocabulary words. Use them at home whenever you can.

alike/same	color	different
set	shape	size
sort/classify		

Book Corner

Next time you visit the library, check out one of these books:
Accorsi, William. *Billy's Button*. Greenwillow, 1992.
Hoban, Tana. *Is It Red? Is It Yellow? Is It Blue?* Greenwillow, 1987.
___. *Is It Rough? Is It Smooth? Is It Shiny?* Greenwillow, 1984.
Lionni, Leo. *Little Blue and Little Yellow*. Astor-Honor, 1959.

This page may be copied and sent home to parents.

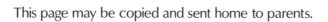

Chapter 4

Patterning

Definition

A pattern is a repetition of a designated item (color, block, crayon, book) or group of items. Patterns occur naturally everywhere in the environment. We are surrounded by patterns in nature, in clothing, in music and in written text. Patterns can be created, copied and extended.

Bridge to Other Math Concepts

Children will need the ability to recognize attributes of specific items, to name those attributes and identify similarities and differences before they are ready to work with patterns. Recognizing, copying, extending and creating patterns will help children develop an awareness of sequence which is necessary before understanding skip counting, odd and even numbers and ordering. Copying patterns also begins an unconscious recognition of one-to-one correspondence.

Suggestions for Success

◆ Begin patterning with concrete objects like the children themselves. Then move to more abstract concepts like music patterns and text patterns.
◆ It's easy to move too quickly with patterning concepts. Be sure children have internalized copying patterns before you ask them to extend or create patterns.
◆ If you use geometric shapes for activities in this chapter, which is natural, remember to focus on their appearance only and not on their specific attributes (number of sides and corners). We will introduce shapes and their attributes in Chapter 8, after children have been introduced to numbers.
◆ Do Activities 1-21 using simple AB patterns (red block/green block, red block/green block; or fish cracker/butterfly cracker, fish cracker/butterfly cracker). Then repeat the activities using more complex patterns like AAB (red block, red block, green block/ red block, red block, green block) or ABC (red block, green block, yellow block/ red block, green block, yellow block). Continue through the chapter letting children use both simple and complex patterns.

Key Words

before	beginning	circular
continue	copy	create
end	extend	next
pattern	repeat	

Circle Time Story:
Christmas Decorations Solution

Materials

string of red and green Christmas lights or red and green beads on a string (use
  stringing beads or lights as story props)

Mr. and Mrs. Squirrel looked around their tree house and smiled. All the
Christmas decorations were in place and the spirit of Christmas filled the
house. The stockings were hung at the foots of the beds and the tree was
adorned with berries and nuts.

"Good job," said Mr. Squirrel.

"You know what I'd like to do this year?" said Mrs. Squirrel. "I'd like to put lights
outside."

"Okay," said Mr. Squirrel. "I'll get the lights!"

"Let's use a red, green pattern," said Mrs. Squirrel.

"Oh, no," said Mr. Squirrel. "Green, red looks much better."

"Now, Dear, I assure you red, green is the perfect pattern," said Mrs. Squirrel.

Mr. and Mrs. Squirrel continued to argue for quite a long time. Finally the children
came to see what on earth was going on.

When they heard what the problem was, they started to laugh. They whispered back
and forth to each other and then they said, "We'll do the lights. You stay inside."

The children went outside and put the lights around the tree house. Then they
called their parents to come outside and see the lights.

When Mr. and Mrs. Squirrel saw the lights they each breathed a sigh of relief and
said, "See I told you I knew best!"

Do you know the children's secret?

Materials for Story Extension

red and green stringing beads

Activity

Let the children take the stringing beads outside and experiment with them
on a real tree. If a real tree is not available, string the beads on a tree drawn on
a bulletin board or taped to a wall.

2   We Patterns

Materials

Activity

Create patterns with children. Select six to eight children to help create AB patterns. Try all of the following: standing/sitting, facing forward/facing back, hands up/hands down, girl/boy. What other patterns can you create? Encourage the children to name or describe each one.

3   Patterns Around Me

Materials

Activity

Invite the children to look around the classroom for patterns. Check for patterns in floor tiles or carpet; table and chair arrangements; wallpaper, paint or paneling; book arrangements and so on.

4   Pattern Stuff

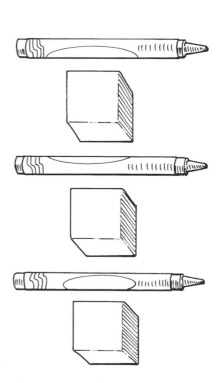

Materials

assortment of objects (crayons, paint-brushes, blocks, plastic animals, etc.)

Activity

Make simple patterns with the objects (block/brush, block/brush or crayon/brush, crayon/brush). Place the objects on a table, chalk tray or floor where children can easily see them. Ask the children to name or describe the patterns.

**5**

Patterns On Me

Materials

Activity

Encourage children to look for patterns in their clothing. Help them see the patterns in plaids, stripes, floral and other prints, polka dots and so on.

**6**

Auditory Patterns

Materials

Activity

Make simple rhythm patterns, such as clap/clap or clap/stomp. Encourage the children to listen for each pattern and describe it.

**7**

Nature Patterns

Materials

natural objects children have collected

Activity

Make patterns from the natural objects the children collected during a walk. You might have leaves of different colors and shapes, twigs and rocks or other objects. Encourage children to talk about and describe the patterns.

8 Outside Patterns

Materials

Activity

Take the children on a nature walk to look for patterns in the environment. Children may find rows of flowers, a wasp's nest, a spider's web or patterns in tree bark or leaf arrangements. Ask children to point out any patterns they find. Ask the children to collect natural objects during their walk for use in later activities. Remind them to take just a little bit and only those things that won't disturb an animal's life or hurt any living thing.

9 Your Turn, My Turn

Materials

recordings of echo songs, optional

Activity

Sing a familiar echo song with the children. (Ella Jenkins has echo songs on several of her recordings, such as "You'll Sing a Song and I'll Sing a Song.") The pattern is my turn/your turn, my turn/your turn. Help the children recognize the AB pattern.

10 Magnetic Patterns

Materials

dowel (stand it in clay)
several magnets with holes drilled through
   the center
spray paint, optional, with adult help

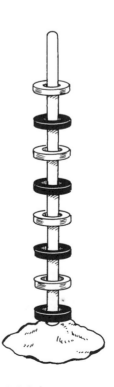

Activity

Encourage children to slide the magnets onto the dowel rod one at a time to create a pattern of magnet/space, magnet/space or magnet, magnet/space. Spaces will be formed by the magnets repelling each other. Or spray paint the magnets to create a color pattern.

11 Left/Right

Materials
recorded march music

Activity
Play a recording of march music and lead the children in marching around the room. Lead them to see the left/right (AB) foot patterns. You might want to place red (left) and blue (right) footprints on the floor to make the pattern more obvious. (Trace around a pair of the children's shoes to make a pattern.)

 COPYING PATTERNS

ACTIVITIES **12** TO **21**

12 Copy Cats

Materials
none

Activity
Use four children to create a pattern (tongue in/tongue out, stand/squat, etc.). Ask the rest of the class to copy what they see. Repeat several times using other patterns.

13 Hands-On Patterning

Materials
manipulatives (color tiles, color blocks, stringing beads, large marbles, etc.)

Activity
Arrange the manipulatives in simple patterns. Encourage the children to copy the patterns.

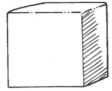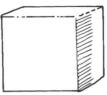

14 That's Mine

Materials

tape recorder and blank tape, optional

Activity

Create an auditory pattern (shhh/boom, cluck/clack, etc.). Encourage the children to join in and continue the pattern. Repeat the activity several times, making up other auditory patterns. Record and play back the patterns, if desired.

15 Color Copies

Materials

paper
markers or crayons
tracing paper

Activity

Draw simple color patterns on sheets of paper. Provide tracing paper and crayons or markers for the children to trace the patterns.

16 Patterned Chains

Materials

1" x 4" strips of construction paper
   (two colors)
glue, tape or stapler

Activity

Make a paper chain (1" x 4" strips of construction paper glued into circles and looped through each other) using two colors of paper. Provide materials for children to copy the pattern.

17 Reflections

Materials
easel and paper
markers or crayons

Activity
Draw a simple pattern at the top of a sheet of easel paper (alternate colors or shapes). Encourage the children to copy the pattern on the bottom of the paper.

18 Anything Patterns

Materials
materials from junk boxes (buttons, bolts, lids, etc.)

Activity
Use the junk box materials to create patterns for children to copy.

19 Chair Patterns

Materials
classroom chairs

Activity
Make a pattern with classroom chairs (red chair/blue chair, facing forward/facing back, etc.) and let children copy the pattern.

20 Flannel Board Copies

Materials
flannel board
felt cutouts

Activity
Create a pattern with colored felt cutouts on the flannel board and invite children to copy the pattern.
Note: Try all activities 1-21 again, using more complex patterns like ABB, AABB, ABC, and so on. See page 87 for an explanation of simple and complex patterns.

21   **Twin Towers**

Materials
blocks

Activity
Build a structure in the block center using a simple pattern and let children create structures copying the pattern you used.

 EXTENDING PATTERNS

ACTIVITIES 22 TO 31

  22   **Who Comes Next?**

Materials
none

Activity
Ask two children to demonstrate a simple pattern such as stand/sit. Call on the remainder of the class to come one at a time and take the appropriate position to extend the pattern. After all the children have taken their places, ask whether anyone can think of a way to continue extending the pattern (going to another classroom, asking you or other adults to join).

23 Around We Go

Materials

Activity

Invite the children to sit in a circle. Start a simple auditory pattern, such as stomp/clap or clap/hum, and invite the children to continue it. Do it again. This time ask the children to continue the pattern one at a time, moving around the circle.

24 Classroom Patterns

Materials

classroom objects (crayons, blocks, etc.)

Activity

Start a simple pattern, placing the objects on a table or chalk tray, and invite children to continue it.

25 Squares Line Up

Materials

4" squares cut from construction paper (use two colors)
glue
butcher paper

Activity

Paste construction paper squares in a simple pattern on a piece of butcher paper. Provide the children with more squares and glue and encourage them to continue the pattern.

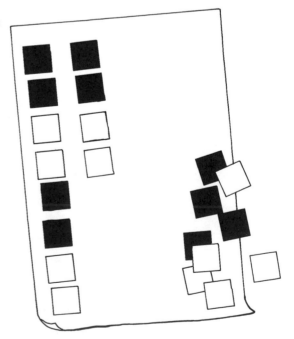

26 **Silly Beads**

Materials

classroom manipulatives
string, optional

Activity

Start a pattern with manipulatives and let children extend it. Just for fun, you might want to hang a string from the ceiling, string on two beads to start a pattern and then let children extend it, pushing the beads up to add on.

 27 **Wall to Wall**

Materials

blocks
crayons

Activity

Start a simple pattern with the blocks at one side of the classroom. Let the children see if they can extend the pattern all the way across the room. Try the activity with crayons. How far can they go?

 28 **Handprints Galore**

Materials

two colors of fingerpaints, each one in a shallow container
large piece of paper

Activity

Use two colors of fingerpaint to begin a handprint pattern on the art table and let children extend it.

29   Flannel Board Extensions

Materials
flannel board
felt cutouts

Activity
Start a pattern with colored felt cutouts on the flannel board and invite children to extend it.

30   Building Patterns

Materials
plastic interlocking blocks, such as Legos

Activity
Start a tower with a two-color pattern. Encourage children to extend the pattern.

31   Follow Those Tracks

Materials
butcher paper   red tempera paint
blue tempera paint   two shallow pans
tub of clean water   towels

Activity
Place a 12' sheet of butcher paper on the floor. Place the two shallow pans at one end. Put red paint in one and blue paint in the other. Invite the children to step barefoot into the paints then walk down the paper, creating a red foot/blue foot pattern. Set the tub of water and towels at the far end of the paper for feet cleaning.

 CREATING PATTERNS

ACTIVITIES **32** TO **41**

32   Children Patterns

Materials

Activity

Let the children create simple patterns with themselves. Encourage them to explain the patterns they create.

33 Easel Variations

Materials

easels
paints

paper
brushes and sponges

Activity

Provide easel paints and encourage the children to create patterns using different colors of paint, different brush widths and different shaped sponges. Ask them to describe their patterns.

34 Window Streamers

Materials

crepe paper streamers
tape

Activity

Provide crepe paper streamers of different colors cut in 18″ lengths. Invite the children to tape the streamers to a wall or window in a pattern they create. You might also cut one or two colors of streamers in two different lengths. Encourage the children to use length and/or color in their patterns.

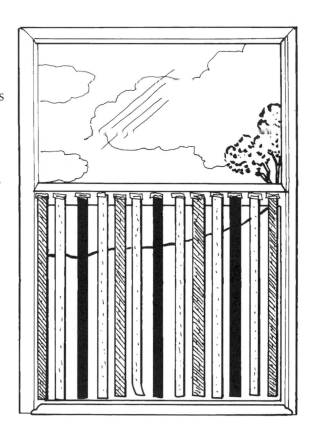

35 Boxes, Boxes

Materials

cardboard boxes and tubes

Activity

Fill the block center with cardboard boxes and tubes for the children to make patterns.

36 Big Patterns

Materials

classroom furniture
assorted materials

Activity

Encourage the children to create patterns using classroom furniture and/or other materials (manipulatives, crayons, blocks, etc.).

37 Edible Patterns

Materials

assorted fruits
wooden skewers
utensils

Activity

Provide a variety of fruits for the children to make patterned fruit kabobs. Orange sections, strawberries, melon balls and banana slices are easy to work with.

38   Musical Repertoire

Materials
rhythm instruments

Activity
Encourage the children to create simple sound patterns with rhythm instruments. Invite them to try simple tone patterns using a xylophone, keyboard or other musical instruments.

39   Say It Again, Sam

Materials
none

Activity
Invite the children to create simple auditory or clapping patterns.

40   Playdough Patterns

Materials
two or more colors of playdough

Activity
Invite the children to make patterns with playdough. They might want to base their patterns on color, size or shape.

41   Shadow Patterns

Materials
overhead projector
assorted materials (pennies, beads, crayons, etc.)

Activity
Encourage children to create shadow patterns by placing items on the overhead projector. Let other children name the pattern.

42   Spoolers

Materials

crepe paper streamers in
  two colors
wire clothes hanger

Activity

Roll up four 8' lengths of
crepe paper (two lengths
of each color). Open the
clothes hanger and slide
the rolled crepe paper, in
an AB pattern, over the
wire. Hang the hanger and,
one by one, unroll the
crepe paper to reveal a
unique pattern.

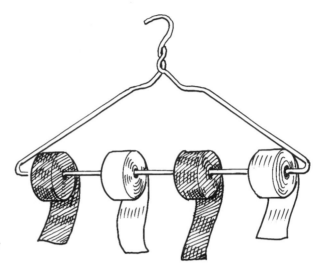

43   Any Which Way

Materials

clear canister (the kind
  tennis balls come in)
playdough balls (two
  colors)

Activity

Place playdough balls
inside the canister
(alternate two colors).
Hold the can horizon-
tally and ask the chil-
dren to describe the
pattern. Turn the can
so that it stands and
ask the children if the
pattern is the same.

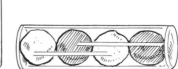
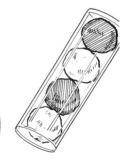

44   Stretchers

Materials

paper-towel tubes
colored rubber bands

Activity

Invite the children to create patterns of colored rubber bands on empty paper-towel tubes.

45   Can Towers

Materials

empty vegetable cans

Activity

Stack vegetable cans in the dramatic play center to make vertical patterns. Encourage the children to copy and extend your pattern and then create their own.

46   Totems

Materials

toilet paper tubes
contact paper or crayons and markers
broom

Activity

Color empty toilet paper tubes or cover them with contact paper. Encourage the children to help. Slide them over a broom handle in simple patterns.

47   Circle, Circle

Materials

classroom chairs

Activity

Invite the children to help you arrange a circle of classroom chairs in a simple pattern.

Colorful Streamers

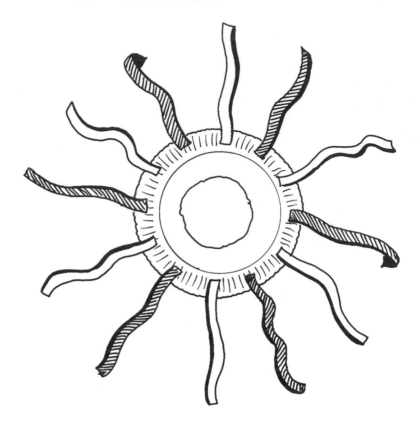

Materials

paper plates
scissors
music

18" streamers of two or three colors
glue

Activity

Cut the centers out of the paper plates. Encourage the children to glue the streamers around their plates in a circular color pattern. Use the "streamer plates" with music for dancing.

49 Wedge Patterns

Materials

construction paper
scissors

Activity

Cut circles of construction paper into pie-shaped wedges. Encourage the children to mix and match colors and create circular patterns.

50　Beads and Laces

Materials

stringing beads and laces

Activity

Encourage the children to string the beads to make circular patterns. You might want to read or tell the opening story again.

51　'Round We Go

Materials

round pizza boards
colored clothespins or paper clips

Activity

Give the children round pizza boards. Encourage children to attach the colored clothespins or paper clips around the boards to create circular patterns.

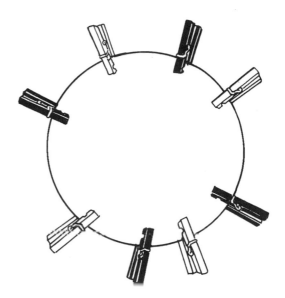

52　Straw Necklaces

Materials

two colors of straws
scissors
yarn

Activity

Cut the straws into 1" lengths. Give children the straw sections and lengths of yarn. Invite them to create a pattern as they string the straw sections onto the yarn and make necklaces.

53

Patterns Around Me

Materials

paper
crayons

Activity

Take a walk around the school and see how many patterns you can find on the building (windows, bricks) or in the yard (shrubs and plants). Let the children take paper and crayons to make rubbings of patterns they find.

 54

Wrap-Arounds

Materials

poster board
marker
natural items the children
    have collected or class-
    room objects

Activity

Make wrap-around patterns. Use a poster board to create a 16-square grid. Let children place items in the squares to make and extend a pattern. Show them how to use three items so the patterns will wrap around.

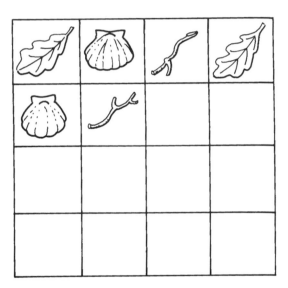

 55

Damp Sand Patterns

Materials

sandbox full of sand

Activity

Dampen the sand in the sandbox. Encourage children to step in the sand with their shoes on, then examine the patterns the soles of their shoes formed in the sand. (Many tennis shoes have very interesting soles.) Invite children to take their shoes off and create left/right patterns with their bare feet.

56   # Rub a Pattern

Materials
leaves
crayons
paper

Activity
Encourage the children to make leaf patterns, then use crayons to rub the patterns onto drawing paper.

 57   # Stamp a Pattern

Materials
rubber stamps
ink pads
paper

Activity
Provide rubber stamps and ink pads for the children to stamp patterns on adding machine paper or other paper.

58   Post-it Patterns

Materials
colored Post-it notes

Activity
Use colored Post-it notes to demonstrate different patterned arrangements (AB, ABC, AAB, etc.). Invite the children to copy your patterns and create their own. See page 87 for a description of AB, ABC and AAB patterns.

 CHALLENGING AND COMPLEX PATTERNS

ACTIVITIES 59 TO 65

59   Over and Under

Materials
two medium-sized balls

Activity
Divide the children into two teams and give each team a ball. Ask each team to form a straight line, one child behind the other. Encourage children to pass the ball from the front of the line to the back by passing it hand to hand between their legs. Have them pass the ball back to the front by passing it hand to hand over their heads. For a more interesting game (and pattern), encourage the children to alternate passing the ball: one child passes it under, the next passes it over.

60   Weave a Pattern

Materials
crepe paper
milk crates

Activity
Make woven patterns. Encourage the children to weave strips of colored crepe paper in milk crates.

More Weaving

Materials

8" x 11" pieces of cardboard
elastic
stapler
Styrofoam meat trays
strips of ribbon, lace and yarn

Activity

Staple four or five pieces of
elastic across each piece of
cardboard. (Tape over any
sharp edges.) Encourage
children to weave strips of
ribbon, lace and yarn through
the elastic.

Cut four or five notches in
opposite ends of the meat
trays. Stretch yarn across the
trays, using the notches to
hold it in place, and tie the ends together in the back. Encourage children to weave
strips of ribbon, lace and yarn through the yarn.

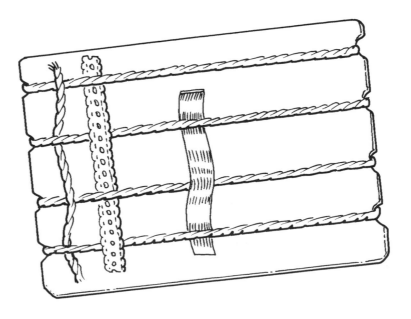

62 ## Story Patterns

Materials

favorite stories and poems
drawings on page 256, optional

Activity

Tell the children familiar stories, such as "The Little Red Hen," "The Three Bears" and "The Three Little Pigs." Encourage children to find the patterns in the stories ("Who will help me?" "Not I.").

 63 ## Wallpaper Favorites

Materials

wallpaper samples

Activity

Provide a variety of wallpaper samples and fabrics. Encourage the children to look for patterns. How many can they find?

 64 ## What's Missing?

Materials

color tiles or other manipulative

Activity

Create a pattern with color tiles or a similar manipulative, then remove random tiles. Have the children determine which tiles are missing.

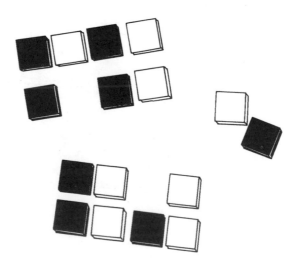

Through the Looking Glass

Materials

natural objects and photographs of natural objects (shells, rocks, toadstools, leaves, flowers, wasp nest, caterpillar, butterfly, spider web, etc.)
magnifying glasses
ink pad and paper, optional

Activity

Encourage children to use the magnifying glasses to examine the objects and pictures you've collected. Invite them to make fingerprints on the paper and examine them, too. What kinds of patterns can the children find?

Any Time Ideas

◆ Create walking patterns when moving from one place to another (hop/skip/jump, big step/little step). Encourage the children to follow your lead, then invite them to take turns leading.
◆ Talk about patterns in days of the week and in seasons when appropriate. For example, school five days/off two days, school five days/off two days, and so on.
◆ Encourage children to arrange themselves in a pattern when lining up to go to the restroom, lunch, outside or any other place that requires a line.

Suggestions for Home Involvement

◆ Ask families to dress their children in clothing that illustrates an easy to identify pattern such as stripes.
◆ Send home a copy of Home Connections on page 113.

Observations and Evaluations

◆ Lay out a simple pattern, using classroom manipulatives or other familiar objects, and ask children to describe the pattern. If children cannot accomplish this, repeat Activities 2-11.
◆ Display a simple pattern and ask children to copy the pattern. If children cannot accomplish this, repeat Activities 12-21.
◆ Create a simple pattern and ask children to extend the pattern. If children cannot accomplish this, repeat Activities 22-31.
◆ Ask children to create a simple pattern. If children cannot accomplish this, repeat Activities 32-41.
◆ Have children do all of the above activities using more complex patterns.

Resources

Children's Books

Brett, Jan. *Goldilocks and the Three Bears.* Putnam, 1989.
Hoban, Tana. *Dots, Spots, Speckles, and Stripes.* Greenwillow, 1987.
Martin, Bill Jr. *Polar Bear, Polar Bear, What Do You Hear?* Holt, 1991.

Records and Songs

Jenkins, Ella. "You'll Sing a Song and I'll Sing a Song." *You'll Sing a Song and I'll Sing a Song.* Folkways.
Lucky, Sharron. "The Three Little Piglets." *Color Me a Rainbow.* Melody House.
Millang, Steve and Greg Scelsa. "Rhyme Time." *Kidding Around with Greg and Steve.* Youngheart.
"Head, Shoulders, Knees, and Toes" and "Apples and Bananas." *Where Is Thumbkin?* Kimbo.

Home Connections

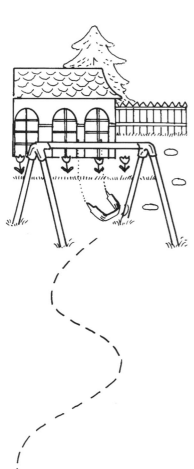

What's New?   Patterning!

Patterns are all around us. We are surrounded by patterns in nature, in clothing, in music and in written text. Recognizing, copying, extending and creating patterns help children develop an awareness of sequence that will help them understand more advanced concepts such as skip counting, odd and even numbers and ordering. Copying patterns also begins an understanding of one-to-one correspondence.

Fun and Easy Things You Can Do at Home

◆ Look for patterns in the fabrics of your clothes, tablecloths and furniture covers.
◆ Encourage your child to make patterns with cookies or crackers before eating them.
◆ Look for patterns in nature like flower petals, tree rings, zebra stripes and so on.

Vocabulary Builders

These are some of our vocabulary words. Use them at home whenever you can.

before	beginning
end	next
pattern	repeat

Book Corner

Next time you visit the library, check out one of these books:
Brett, Jan. *Goldilocks and the Three Bears*. Putnam, 1989.
Hoban, Tana. *Dots, Spots, Speckles, and Stripes*. Greenwillow, 1987.
Martin, Bill Jr. *Polar Bear, Polar Bear, What Do You Hear?* Holt, 1991.

This page may be copied and sent home to parents.

Chapter 5

One-to-One Correspondence

Definition

One-to-one correspondence is matching or pairing items in a one-to-one relationship.

Bridge to Other Math Concepts

In this chapter, children will practice matching items one to one. These activities will lead children naturally into ordering sets (arranging sets according to size). Matching and pairing items helps children to practice, develop and internalize accurate vocabulary. Understanding terms like greater than, less than and equivalent lays a foundation for skills children will need when they begin working with numbers. Understanding one-to-one correspondence will prevent counting errors that occur when children tick off an item more than once or skip an item altogether.

Suggestions for Success

◆ As children begin to match objects, encourage them to describe what they are doing by repeating the pattern phrase, "one ___ for every ___ and one ___ for every ___ ." Two examples are one (napkin) for every (child) and one (child) for every (napkin), one (hat) for every (head) and one (head) for every (hat).
◆ Ask questions to lead children into discussions that will help them make set comparisons. For example, "Are the sets equal?" "Does one set have fewer than another?" or "Is one set greater than another?"

Key Words

equal	equal to
equivalent	fewer
fewer than	greater
greater than	less
less than	member
more	more than
one to one	pair
same	set

Circle Time Story:
A Snowman of My Own

Materials

construction paper cutouts to make snowmen
three small, three medium, and three large circles of white construction paper
orange construction paper nose
brown construction paper stick nose
coal nose, licorice mouth, top hat of black construction paper
red construction paper mouth, one cherry size and another apple size
hats that resemble a beach hat and baseball cap, cut out of any color
   construction paper

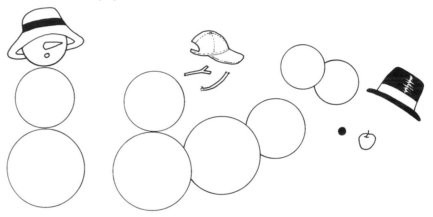

One day Megin and Sam and their friend Justin were building a snowman. Megin rolled a big round ball for the bottom of the snowman. Sam rolled a medium size ball for the middle of the snowman. Justin rolled a small ball for the snowman's head. The snowman was really starting to look like a snowman.

"Now we need some eyes," said Justin. Sam reached into his pocket and pulled out two pieces of coal. The children placed the eyes on their snowman's face.

"Let's use this carrot for his nose," said Megin.

"No," said Sam. "Let's use a stick."

"A stick is too thin," said Justin. "Let's use more coal."

The children began talking all at one time, each trying to describe the reasons his or her idea was best.

Megin's and Sam's mother, Kathy, heard the children arguing. She went to the front porch and asked the children to come discuss their problem with her. "How can we solve this problem?" asked Kathy.

The children began to think. Megin suggested making a snowman with three noses. The other children laughed. Justin thought perhaps the children could change the snowman's nose each day. "Too much trouble," said Megin.

Finally, Sam began to jump up and down and shout, "I've got it! I've got a good idea! We can each build our own snowman. One snowman for every child and one child for every snowman."

"That sounds like a great idea," said the other children.

Megin gave her snowman a carrot nose, a cherry mouth and a floppy beach hat. Sam gave his a nose made from a stick, a mouth of licorice and a baseball cap. Justin's snowman had a nose made out of coal, an apple mouth and his dad's best top hat.

"What wonderful snowmen," said Kathy. She took a picture of the children standing by their snowmen. "Now," she said, "we have one snowman for every child and one child for every snowman, a perfect match!"

Materials for Story Extension

construction paper cutouts used to tell the story

Activity

Place the cutouts in the language center and let the children recreate the story.

 MATCHING EVEN SETS

 2 **Pairs**

Materials

ice cube tray
pairs of small objects (buttons, nuts, bolts, color tiles, etc.)

Activity

Encourage the children to arrange the objects in pairs in the tray sections.

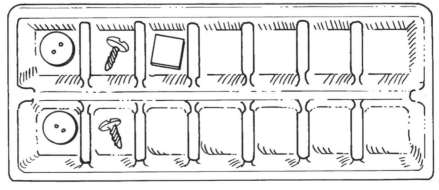

3 # Mixed Up Match

Materials

children's gloves, mittens or shoes

Activity

At circle time invite the children to toss all their gloves, mittens or shoes in the center of the circle. Ask them to help mix them all up. Then encourage the children to match the items one to one to recreate the pairs.

 4 # Working Pairs

Materials

drumsticks, chopsticks, roller blades, stilts, skis, all optional

Activity

Encourage the children to brainstorm a list of things you need two of to work or do something (drumsticks, chopsticks, roller blades, stilts, skis, etc.). If they are available, demonstrate using some of the items. You can make a pair of stilts using two large coffee cans with rope handles.

 5 # Concentration

Materials

index cards made into a Concentration Game (use shapes, colors or animal drawings on page 253)

Activity

Invite the children to play Concentration. Point out the one-to-one match.

6 **You Must Have Been a Beautiful Baby**

Materials

baby picture and current picture of each child (ask families to provide them)
yarn

Activity

Put the photos on a bulletin board where everyone can see them. Encourage the children to match their baby picture with their current photograph. Let them use lengths of yarn to connect the two.

 7 **Matching Game**

Materials

color tiles, candies, and/or buttons

Activity

Put pairs of color tiles, candies and/or buttons in a sack. (Total number should match number of children. Join the group, if necessary, to make an even number.) Encourage each child to draw an object from the sack, then find a friend who has a matching object.

 8 **Go Togethers**

Materials

nuts and bolts
jars with lids
shirts with buttons

Activity

Encourage the children to match nuts to bolts, lids to jars and buttons to button-holes.

9 Where Is Thumbkin?

Materials

Activity

Invite the children to sing "Where Is Thumbkin?" and perform the hand motions. Make sure children see the one-to-one relationship of the thumbs and fingers on their hands.

Where is thumbkin? (start with fists behind back)
Where is thumbkin?
Here I am, (bring out right thumb)
Here I am; (bring out left thumb)
How are you today, sir? (wiggle right thumb)
Very well, I thank you. (wiggle left thumb)
Run away, run away. (put fists behind back)

Where is pointer?
Where is middle finger?
Where is ring finger?
Where is pinky?

10 One Peg for Every Hole

Materials

pegboard and pegs

Activity

Invite the children to arrange the pegs in the board any way they want. Point out the one-to-one correspondence of pegs to holes. Use the phrase "one peg for every hole, one hole for every peg."

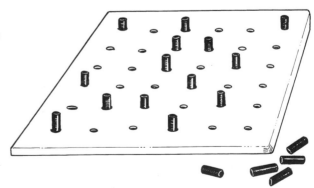

11   Copy Cat Towers

Materials

blocks

Activity

Invite children to work in pairs. Give each pair two identical sets of blocks. Ask one of each pair to build a tower, giving block-by-block instructions to the partner for copying the tower.

12   Dance

Materials

Activity

Invite children to stand in a circle (join them if necessary for an even number). Ask partners to face each other as children chant this chant:

Bow wow wow (point alternating index fingers at partner)
Who's dog are thou? (point alternating index fingers at partner)
Little Tommy Tucker's dog (jump up, turn around to face new partner)
Bow wow wow (stomp alternating feet three times)

Repeat, turning back and forth between two partners. Point out the one-to-one correspondence of partner to partner, fingers to fingers, feet to feet.

13   Pat-a-Cake

Materials

Activity

Invite the children to choose partners and play pat-a-cake games. Point out the one-to-one correspondence of child to child and hands to hands.

14   Three Bears

Materials

favorite version of "The Three Bears"
props (stuffed bears, bowls, chairs, etc.) or flannel board and cutouts made using
    drawings on page 256

Activity

Tell the children the story of the Three Bears. Use the props or flannel board
pieces to help. Afterwards, encourage children to match props to bears. They
might want to retell the story.

15   Who's Here?

Use one of the following ways to mark children's attendance each day. Point out
the one-to-one correspondence, using the pattern phrase.

Materials

tongue depressors or craft sticks
photo of each child
two cans

Activity

Attach a small photograph of each child to a tongue depressor or craft stick. Put
all the sticks in one can. Set an empty can next to it. As the children come in each
morning, ask them to move their photo sticks from one can to the other.

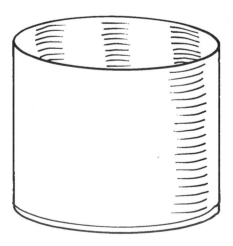

Materials

name cards
pocket chart

Activity

Invite the children to write their names on cards and then decorate them. Hang up a pocket chart for the children to put their cards in as they come in each day.

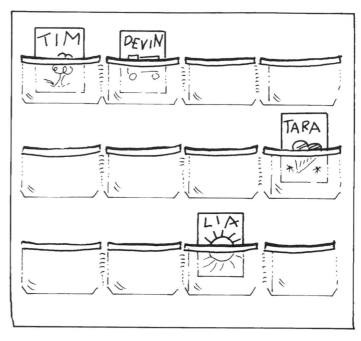

Materials

clothespins
large can or
    bucket

Activity

Give each child a clothespin to decorate. Write the children's names on the clothespins. Put the clothespins in a large can or bucket. As the children come in, encourage them to pick out their clothespin and pin it to the side of the bucket.

Materials

key tags
photo of each child
pegboard and hooks

Activity

Put a photo of each child on a key tag. Draw a happy face on the opposite side of each tag. Hang all the tags on pegboard hooks. As children come in each day, ask them to flip their tags over to show the happy face.

 16

Set the Table

Materials

place mats
dishes
utensils

Activity

Draw plate, cup and utensil outlines on several place mats. Place them in the dramatic play center with dishes and utensils. Encourage children to set the table.

 17

Shakers

Materials

film canisters
tweezers
small beads or seeds

Activity

Encourage the children to pick up a bead or seed with tweezers and place it in a canister. Continue until every canister has a bead or button inside. Put the lids on the canisters and use them as rhythm instruments during music time.

18   Find a Friend

Materials

one photograph of each child
folder
glue

Activity

Make two photocopies of each photograph. Glue one set of pictures inside the folder in a board game format. Laminate the other set to make photo cards. Invite children to match the photo cards to the photos glued inside the folder.

19   Rings on My Fingers

Materials

ten plastic rings

Activity

Encourage children to put a ring on each finger. Point out the one-to-one correspondence, modeling the language "One ring for every finger, one finger for every ring."

20   Anything You Can Do. . .

Materials

classroom objects (crayons, blocks, etc.)

Activity

Build a set of objects and encourage the children to create a matching set. For example, lay five crayons in a row and encourage children to lay a matching set below yours.

21 One Brush for Every Jar

Materials

paint jars
paintbrushes

Activity

Set out several paint jars. Encourage children to match brushes to the paint jars.
Ask children to think about what would happen if there were more paint jars than
brushes. How would that affect their painting? What if there were more brushes
than paint jars?

22 Puzzle Box Match-up

Materials

shoe box
marker
knife
assortment of small objects (crayon, spoon, puzzle piece, block, etc.)

Activity

Trace several small objects on the lid of a shoe box, then cut out the shapes.
Encourage children to put the objects through their matching cutouts. When all the
objects are in the box, ask children to remove the lid and lay it on a table.
Encourage them to lay the objects on the lid, matching objects to cutouts.

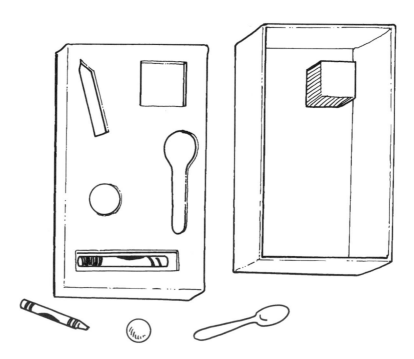

23   ## Pie Slices

Materials

paper plates
clothespins

colored stick-on dots
colored tape

Activity

Draw lines across two paper plates, dividing each into eight equal wedges. Cut one plate apart. Encourage children to match cutout wedges to those on the other plate. Put matching colored stick-on dots on the wedges and the sections on the uncut plate. Encourage children to place the wedges on the sections by matching the colored dots. You can also put colored tape on clothespins and encourage children to match the color on each clothespin to one of the colored dots on the plate.

 MATCHING UNEVEN SETS

ACTIVITIES **24** TO **31**

 24   ## Take a Seat

Materials

classroom chairs

Activity

Encourage the children to match themselves to classroom chairs. Are there enough chairs for everyone to have a seat? Are there chairs left over?

 25   ## Musical Chairs

Materials

classroom chairs
music

Activity

Encourage the children to play Musical Chairs. Point out the one-to-one correspondence between children and chairs.

26 ## Visiting Class

Materials
none

Activity
Encourage children to match themselves one to one with the children in another class. How does it turn out? Does one class have more children than the other?

 27 ## Boys to Girls

Materials
none

Activity
Encourage the children to match boys and girls in the class one to one. Are the sets even? Are there boys left over? Girls?

 28 ## Gingerbread People

Materials
M&Ms
cutouts in the shape of gingerbread people

Activity
Divide the children into groups of four. Give each group a cutout and a handful of M&Ms. Invite the children to decorate their cutouts with the candies. When they're finished, ask the children to look at all the decorated cutouts and tell which one they would most like to eat and why. When they say they've picked the cutout with the most candies, have them test their selection. Encourage the children to use one-to-one correspondence to find out which cutout actually has the most candies.

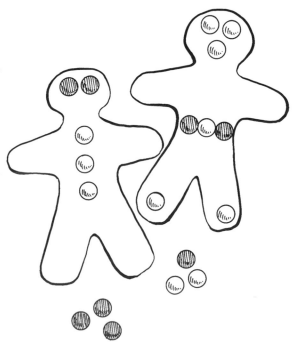

Count on Math

29   Block to Block

Materials

shape blocks or colored inch cubes

Activity

Set up uneven sets of blocks. Encourage children to match the members of the sets one to one and describe the sets. Which has more? Which has fewer? Repeat the activity using other classroom objects.

30   Crayon Match

Materials

crayons in the art center

Activity

Encourage the children to sort the crayons from the art center according to color. Ask them to match the sets one to one. Which sets have more? Are any sets the same?

31   Nature Walk

Materials

natural items children collect

Activity

Invite children on a nature walk. Encourage them to collect items like fallen leaves, pebbles, feathers, twigs, and so on. When you return to the classroom, encourage the children to sort their items into groups, then match members of the sets one to one. Are any sets the same? What items did the children collect the most of?

32   **Favorite Colors**

Materials

one sheet of red construction paper
one sheet of blue construction paper
2″ squares of red and blue

Activity

Lay the red and blue sheets of paper on the floor. Invite the children to line up behind the color they like best. Give each child a corresponding color square. Ask the children to lay their squares on the floor then back away from the line. Encourage them to use one-to-one correspondence to determine the more popular color.

 ## 33   **Favorite Juice**

Materials

two flavors of juice
two colors of paper cups

Activity

Invite the children to ask for the juice they like best. Pour one flavor in one color cup and the other flavor in the other color cup. When children are through drinking, ask them to leave their cups on the table. Encourage children to line up the cups and use one-to-one correspondence to determine the more popular juice.

 ## 34   **Oh, Brother! Oh, Sister!**

Materials

butcher paper or large sheet of drawing paper
marker
blocks

Activity

Draw a line to divide the paper in half. On one side draw a simple stick figure; on the other side draw a stick figure with a line through it. Give each child a block. Invite the children who have a brother to stack their blocks in a tower next to the stick figure. Invite the children who do not have a brother to stack their blocks in a tower near the stick figure with the line through it. Ask children to compare the number of blocks in each tower. Are there more children with a brother or without a brother? Do the activity again, this time creating a graph to show how many children have a sister and how many do not.

Note: Be sensitive to various family configurations.

 35 # Whose Shoes?

Materials

Activity

Ask the children to form two lines. All the children wearing shoes with laces stand in one line. All those wearing shoes without laces to stand in the other. Encourage the children to use one-to-one correspondence to determine which line has more members.

 36 # Apples and Bananas

Materials

picture of an apple   picture of a banana
chart paper   marker

Activity

Divide a sheet of chart paper into two columns. At the top of one column, put a picture of an apple. At the top of the other column, put a picture of a banana. Invite children to make a tally mark under the fruit they like best. Encourage children to use one-to-one correspondence to determine which column has the most tally marks and which fruit is more popular.

37   Wormy Apples

Materials

packing peanuts
drawing on page 254
scissors

Activity

Use the drawing to make five apples. Cut one hole in one apple, two holes in the next, three holes in another and so on. Laminate. Give the children squiggly worms (packing peanuts) to match to the holes in each apple.

38   Shadow Match

Materials

black and white (or manila) construction paper
several familiar objects (block, puzzle piece, scissors, key, can, etc.)
scissors
glue

Activity

Trace around several familiar objects on black construction paper. Cut out each outline and glue it to a sheet of white construction paper. Encourage children to match the objects with their "shadows."

Any Time Ideas

◆ Match children to chairs in the classroom.
◆ Use snack time to compare napkins, cups, cookies and so on with children. Remember to use the pattern phrase, one ____ for every child and one child for every ____.
◆ Use carpet squares to sit on during circle time. Encourage children to check the one-to-one correspondence.

Suggestions for Home Involvement

◆ Give children a ziplock bag with six marbles or pebbles (adjust if you know a child has a larger family). Ask the children to match the marbles or pebbles one to one with each family member, discard the extra pebbles or marbles and bring their bag back to school with one marble or pebble to represent each family member. Compare sets to determine which child comes from the largest family.
◆ Send home a copy of Home Connections on page 134.

Observations and Evaluations

◆ Give children a set of objects (beads, buttons, etc.) and have them match the objects one to one. If children cannot accomplish this, repeat Activities 2-23.

◆ Provide children with two uneven sets of objects and ask them to compare the sets. Have them describe the results. Listen for correct terminology. If children cannot accomplish this, repeat Activities 24-32.

◆ Ask children to create equal and unequal sets. Ask for descriptions and explanations.

Resources

Children's Books

Brett, Jan. *Goldilocks and the Three Bears*. Putnam, 1989.

Hong, Lily Toy. *Two of Everything*. Albert Whitman, 1993.

Martin, Bill Jr. and Archambault, John. *Knots on a Counting Rope*. Holt, 1987.

Miller, Margaret. *Whose Hat?* Greenwillow, 1988.

Zolotow, Charlotte. *Some Things Go Together*. HarperCollins, 1987.

"Three Little Pigs." Many versions available.

Records and Songs

Jenkins, Ella. "Did You Feed My Cow?" *You'll Sing a Song and I'll Sing a Song*. Folkways.

___. "Follow the Leader." *Play Your Instruments and Make a Pretty Sound*. Folkways.

___. "My Echo." *Hopping Around from Place to Place*. Educational Activities.

___. "You'll Sing a Song and I'll Sing a Song." *You'll Sing a Song and I'll Sing a Song*. Folkways.

Lucky Sharron. "The Three Little Piglets." *Color Me a Rainbow*. Melody House.

Millang, Steve and Greg Scelsa. "Little Sir Echo." *We All Live Together, Volume 1*. Youngheart.

"Where Is Thumbkin?" *Where Is Thumbkin?* Kimbo.

Home Connections

What's New?   One-to-One Correspondence!

We are working on one-to-one correspondence and set comparison. Children will practice matching items one to one. They will use this skill to compare sets. These activities will lead children naturally into ordering sets (arranging sets according to size), to begin to understand that five is one more than four, six is one more than five and so on.

Fun and Easy Things You Can Do at Home

◆ Encourage your child to help set the table. Point out the one-to-one correspondence of plates, silverware, glasses, napkins and people.
◆ Ask your child to match pairs of shoes.
◆ When you serve food, talk about how each person gets one piece or one serving. Use the phrase "One piece for you, one piece for me."

Vocabulary Builders

These are some of our vocabulary words. Use them at home whenever you can.

equal	fewer than
more than	one to one
greater than	less than
pair	set

Book Corner

Next time you visit the library, check out one of these books:
Brett, Jan. *Goldilocks and the Three Bears*. Putnam, 1989.
Martin, Bill Jr. and Archambault, John. *Knots on a Counting Rope*. Holt, 1989.
Miller, Margaret. *Whose Hat?* Greenwillow, 1988.
Zolotow, Charlotte. *Some Things Go Together*. HarperCollins, 1987.

This page may be copied and sent home to parents.

Count on Math

Chapter 6

Ordering

Definition

Ordering is organizing and arranging objects and sets of objects using one-to-one correspondence. Ordering helps children understand that numbers have a specific order (fewer to more) and that each number is one more than the number before. Ordering is organizing materials and information in a specific pattern. Sequence is what comes next.

Bridge to Other Math Concepts

When children can compare sets and describe the results, they are ready to place sets in a specified order. Since children have not been introduced to numbers and counting, they will be organizing and arranging sets by using one-to-one correspondence or by noticing that some sets have more or less members than others.

Suggestions for Success

◆ Begin working on order by showing children items they can see as being long, longer and longest or tall, taller and tallest. You might use the children themselves or exaggerated lengths of rope or yarn. Show the children piles of buttons that illustrate few, many and more.

◆ Be sure to provide plenty of practice with both discrete (countable) and continuous (measurable) materials.

◆ As you make comparisons, be sensitive to any situation that may be embarrassing to a child. For example, some children are sensitive about their height (shortest, tallest).

Key Words

big, bigger, biggest
heavy, heavier, heaviest
long, longer, longest
small, medium, large
short, shorter, shortest
top, middle, bottom

first, next, last
light, lighter, lightest
most, least
small, smaller, smallest
tall, taller, tallest

Circle Time Story:
Who Will Choose Me?

Materials

five construction paper hearts of graduated sizes, write on the back of the
smallest valentine, "I LOVE YOU SO MUCH MY HEART IS FULL"

The storekeeper arranged the valentine cards on the shelf. First he put the
cards out in no specific order. Then he backed up and looked at them.
"Hmm," he said. "I'm not sure the cards look their best like this." He scratched his
chin and thought for a minute. Then he moved back to the shelf and put the cards
in order, smallest to largest.

Then the storekeeper moved back again to look at the shelf of cards. "This still
doesn't look right to me," he said.

He went back to the shelf and arranged the valentine cards from largest to smallest. This time when he moved back to look at the shelf, he smiled a smile of
approval. "I like this," he said.

After he left, the valentine cards began to talk among themselves about their
arrangement. "I've got the best position," said the largest valentine. "People will
notice me first. I'll be the first to find a home. Just wait and see."

The next valentine on the shelf was happy, too. She was sure she would be selected as someone's special card. Actually, all the cards were happy with their position except the smallest valentine, who was last.

"I'm already small," said the little valentine. "Here at the end of the line, I'll be really
hard to see."

As people came into the store and looked at the valentines, they always picked up
the larger ones at the front of the line first. And sure enough, the largest valentine
in first place was the first to find a home.

The littlest valentine was starting to worry. He felt tears welling up in his eyes. Just
then a little boy came into the store with his mother. From way across the room he
spied the little valentine. "Oh, Mama, I see the perfect valentine," said the boy. He
ran straight to the little valentine and took it from the shelf.

"Look Mama. This card is just right for baby brother. What does it say, Mama?"
The little boy's mother turned the card over and read the message. "It says, 'I
LOVE YOU SO MUCH MY HEART IS FULL.'"

"See Mama. I knew it was perfect," said the little boy as he took the valentine
from his mother and pressed it to his heart.

The little valentine smiled. He knew he had found the best home of all.

Materials for Story Extension

cut-out hearts of graduated sizes (decorated as desired)

Activity

Place the valentines in the math center and let the children explore putting the cards in different arrangements (smallest to largest, largest to smallest). You can change the story to focus on any type of greeting card.

ORDERING BY SIZE

2 Flannel Board Hearts

Materials

various sizes of hearts cut from red, white and pink felt or faces cut out of paper or felt using the drawings on page 255
flannel board

Activity

Encourage the children to arrange the cut-out hearts (or faces) from smallest to largest and from largest to smallest.

3 Kids in All Sizes

Materials

Activity

Divide the children into sets of four. Encourage children in each set to arrange themselves from shortest to tallest and from tallest to shortest.

4   Balls, Balls, Balls

Materials

assortment of balls (Make sure you have a variety of sizes.)

Activity

Talk about the different sizes of balls. Encourage the children to arrange them from smallest to largest. Help the children think of other things they could arrange in the same way (grocery items on a shelf, books, drinks at a fast-food restaurant, etc.).

5   Playdough Balls

Materials

playdough

Activity

Invite the children to make different-sized balls with the playdough. Encourage them to arrange the balls from smallest to largest and from largest to smallest.

6   Concentric Circles

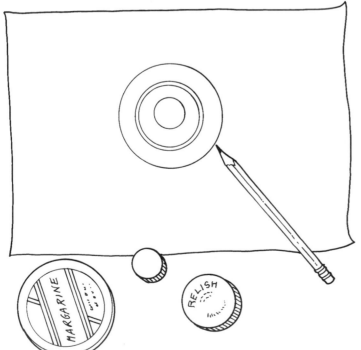

Materials

sheets of paper
pencils
assortment of jar lids

Activity

Show the children how to trace around the jar lids to make circles on the paper. Invite the children to trace around the lids, creating an arrangement of circles from smallest to largest.

7   **Would You Like Fries with That?**

Materials

clean, empty containers from fast food restaurants (drink cups, sandwich boxes, French fry boxes, sacks, etc.)

Activity

Invite the children to arrange the sets of objects from smallest to largest and from largest to smallest. After the lesson, place all the containers in the dramatic play center. Encourage the children to experiment with different arrangements.

8   **Three Bears**

Materials

drawings on page 256
felt
flannel board

Activity

Use the drawings on page 256 to make flannel board pieces. Use the pieces as you tell the story of "The Three Bears." Encourage the children to help with the telling and with the arranging of flannel board pieces. Tell the story again, this time with Goldilocks always trying the smallest things first. Encourage children to arrange the flannel board pieces. Afterwards, invite the children to practice telling the story and arranging the pieces on their own.

9   **Teddy Bear Day**

Materials

stuffed bears (Ask children to bring them from home. Make sure you have some extras on hand for children who forget or who don't have stuffed bears.)

Activity

Invite the children to bring all their bears together and then arrange them from smallest to largest. Encourage children to talk about their arrangement and the placement of the bears. Make the day even more fun by serving porridge (oatmeal) in different sized bowls.

10   Door Frames

Materials

one side of a large card-
board box (refrigerator
size)
duct tape
scissors or sharp knife

Activity

Fit the cardboard over an
open door frame. Attach it
with duct tape. Cut a small
door (2' high x 20" wide)
in the cardboard. The next
day, enlarge the opening to
3' x 22". On the third day,
enlarge the opening to 4' x
24". Encourage the children
to talk about how the size
of the opening changes.

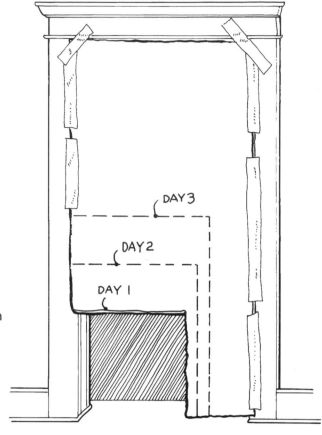

11   Seeds

Materials

a variety of seeds
magnifying glasses

Activity

Invite the children to examine the seeds closely and then arrange
them from largest to smallest.

Tunnels of Fun

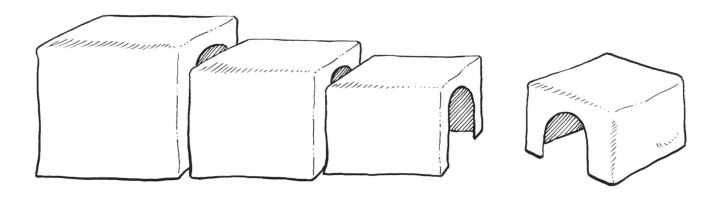

Materials

several large cardboard boxes of varying sizes

Activity

Cut an arch in two sides of each box. Encourage the children to arrange the boxes from largest to smallest, connecting the arches, to make a tunnel. Invite the children to crawl through. Are all the boxes large enough to crawl through? Is anybody stuck? How did it feel to crawl into a smaller and smaller space?

ORDERING BY HEIGHT AND LENGTH

ACTIVITIES 13 TO 21

13 Snow Folk

Materials

real snow, if available, or white playdough (add white tempera paint)

Activity

Invite the children to make balls with the snow or playdough, then use the balls to build snow people. Talk about how children arrange the balls from largest to smallest as they build. When all the snow folk are finished, encourage the children to arrange them all from shortest to tallest.

14   Height and Length

Materials

Activity

Invite four children to stand in front of the class. Encourage the other children to arrange the four from tallest to shortest and from shortest to tallest. Ask the children to brainstorm a list of things they could order according to height. Then ask them to brainstorm a list of things they could order according to length. Help children understand that height applies to vertical objects and length applies to horizontal objects.

15   Everybody's Bodies

Materials

butcher paper
markers
crayons and/or paints

Activity

Invite children to lie on the butcher paper while you trace around their bodies. Encourage the children to color and decorate the silhouettes. Cut out the silhouettes, then ask the children to arrange them from tallest to shortest. Tape the silhouettes in order around the room.

16   Families

Materials

drawing paper
scissors
crayons and/or markers

Activity

For each child, divide a sheet of drawing paper into sections so that you have a section for each member of the child's family. Encourage the children to draw pictures of themselves and their family members, ordered from tallest to shortest, in the sections. Cut the sections apart and let the children experiment with putting their family members into another order.

17   Tall Towers

Materials
blocks

Activity
Give children several blocks each. Model building different towers with your own set of blocks, then ask the children to build their own. Help the children arrange the towers by height from shortest to tallest. Ask them to describe the arrangement. Then, ask the children to reverse the order and describe that arrangement.

18   Size Hunt

Materials
none

Activity
Invite children to go on a Size Hunt. Encourage them to find objects in the classroom that they can order from shortest to tallest or shortest to longest (blocks, hats, crayons, chairs, tables, etc.).

19   Snake Charmers

Materials
playdough

Activity
Provide playdough for the children to make snakes of several different lengths. Ask the children to arrange the snakes from longest to shortest or from shortest to longest.

20 Lengths of Yarn

Materials

yarn cut into 12″ lengths
scissors
paper
glue

Activity

Give each child a piece of yarn, scissors, glue and paper. Encourage children to cut their yarn into smaller pieces and arrange them from shortest to longest on their paper. When they are satisfied with their order, ask the children to glue the yarn pieces onto the paper.

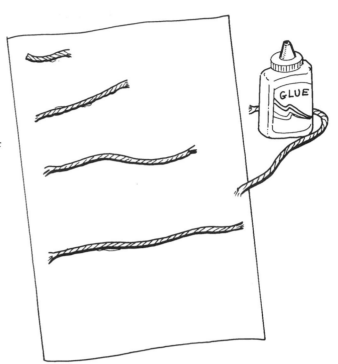

21 Broad Jump

Materials

masking tape
yarn
scissors

Activity

Place a piece of masking tape on the floor. Invite the children one at a time to stand just behind the line and jump as far as they can. Cut a length of yarn to show the length of each jump. Be sure to put masking tape with a mark for identification on the end of each piece of yarn. Take the lengths of yarn outside and encourage the children to put them in order from longest to shortest.

22 Weighted Cans

Materials

blocks, seeds or sand
four or five coffee cans

Activity

Put varying amounts of blocks, seeds or sand in the coffee cans. Encourage the children to arrange the cans from heaviest to lightest and from lightest to heaviest.

23 Balance Scales

Materials

objects
balance scale(s)

Activity

Encourage children to gather two to four objects from around the room. Have children weigh the objects on balance scales and arrange them from lightest to heaviest or heaviest to lightest.

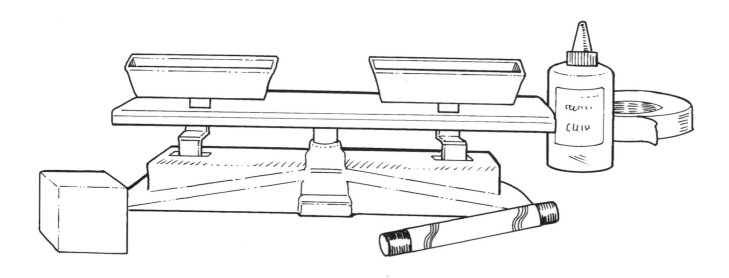

24   A Weighty Issue

Materials

Activity

Encourage the children to brainstorm a list of objects they can weigh. Talk about times when it might be a good idea to arrange objects according to weight (putting the heaviest box on the bottom of a stack and the lightest box on top, balancing weights on a seesaw, etc.).

25   Bungee Scale

Materials

objects of varying weights
bungee cord with a small bucket
    attached to it
butcher paper
marker

Activity

Hang the bungee cord and bucket in front of a wall in the science center. Hang the butcher paper on the wall, directly behind the bucket. Invite the children to place one of the objects inside the bucket. How far does the bucket move? Ask children to put a mark on the butcher paper to show where the bucket hangs. Draw a picture or write the name of the object near the mark. Continue placing the other objects one at a time in the bucket and marking the place. Ask the children to study their findings. Encourage them to arrange the objects according to the marks on the butcher paper.

BLOCK

DOLL

TRUCK

26 Sock It to Me

Materials

objects of different weights (block, paper clip, spool, etc.)
a sock for each object

Activity

Place each object inside a sock. Invite the children to lift each sock, then order the filled socks from lightest to heaviest.

27 Egg Weights

Materials

four plastic eggs
sand
tape

Activity

Fill the eggs with varying amounts of sand and tape them securely. Encourage the children to arrange the eggs according to weight.

ORDERING BY OTHER ATTRIBUTES

ACTIVITIES 28 TO 30

28 Sandy Textures

Materials

sand paper (fine, medium and coarse grades)

Activity

Cut sandpaper into squares. Encourage the children to feel the textures, describe them and arrange them from fine to coarse textures.

29 Rising Waters

Materials

four jars, all the same size   water
measuring cups   food coloring

Activity

Fill the jars with 1/4 cup blue water, 1/2 cup green water, 3/4 cup red water and 1 cup yellow water, respectively. Help children arrange the jars from least amount of water to most amount of water. Rearrange the jars from most water to least water. Discuss the relationship of the water in the jars (the green water is more than the blue, the blue water is less than the red, etc.).

30   Tone Bottles

Materials

six glass bottles
water
stick

Activity

Create a set of tone bottles by varying the amount of water in six glass bottles. Arrange the bottles in order from the a least amount of water to most water. Provide a stick and encourage children to explore the tones made by gently tapping on each bottle. Have the children arrange the bottles from lowest tone to highest. Do they have to move any bottles?

31 Gingerbread Men

Materials

gingerbread men cut from brown construction paper, one for each child
small candies

Activity

Divide children into groups of four. Give each child a gingerbread man and a handful of candies. Encourage the children to use their candies to decorate their gingerbread men. When children are finished, encourage each group to arrange their gingerbread men from those that appear to have the least candies to those that appear to have the most candies. Ask children to think of a way to check their arrangement. Encourage them to match candies one to one. Rearrange if necessary.

32 Graduated Sets

Materials

shower curtain
counters
masking tape

Activity

Divide the counters into five graduated sets (one counter in the first set, two counters in the second set, etc.). Use the masking tape to create a grid with 25 squares on the shower curtain. Encourage children to place each set of counters on one row of squares—one counter to one square. Lead children to see that each set is one more than the set before and one less than the next set.

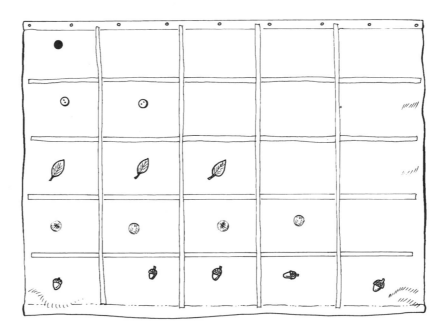

33 Button Grab

Materials
buttons
small bags or sacks

Activity
Divide the children into groups of three and give each group a sack of buttons. Encourage each child to take a handful of buttons from the sack. Then have all the children in each group lay their buttons down and compare the sets using one-to-one correspondence. Encourage the children to arrange their sets of buttons in order from most-to-least or least-to-most.

34 One More

Materials
objects

Activity
Encourage children to create sets of objects to demonstrate one more. Invite one child to start with a set of one or two. Ask another child to create a set of one more and so on.

35 Penny Dots

Materials
sheets of construction paper
pennies
markers

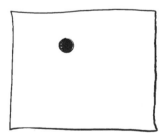  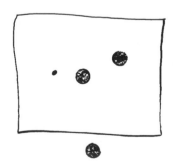 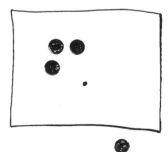

Activity

Lay out four sheets of construction paper. Place one penny on the first sheet of paper, two pennies on the next and so on. Ask the children to tell, without counting, whether the sheets of paper are in order of fewest to most pennies. When children see the fewest-to-most order, take one penny off and make a dot on the paper in its place. Continue removing pennies and making dots. Talk about how each dot represents one penny. After you have removed all the pennies, mix up the sheets of papers. Encourage the children to rearrange them in order from fewest dots to most dots.

36   Dot Cards

Materials

twenty-five index cards
markers

Activity

Make a set of dot cards. Put one dot on five cards, two dots on five cards and so on. Show the cards to the children, then shuffle and stack them face down. Invite one child to draw a card and place it face up. Invite a second child to draw another card and place it face up next to the first card to create a least dots to most dots order. Continue the game, asking children to place the next card in the appropriate place in the arrangement.

37   Follow the Dots

Materials

drawing paper with
    random sets of one to
    five dots on them
pencils

Activity

Let children connect the dots by following the least-to-most arrangements of dots. After they finish, provide crayons and let children make a picture from their lines.

38 Hang the Shirts

Materials

five simple construction paper cut-out shirts
marker
clothesline or yarn
clothespins

Activity

Place one to five dots on each shirt. Encourage children to hang the shirts on the clothesline, arranging them in order from least to most dots.

39 Dot Croquet

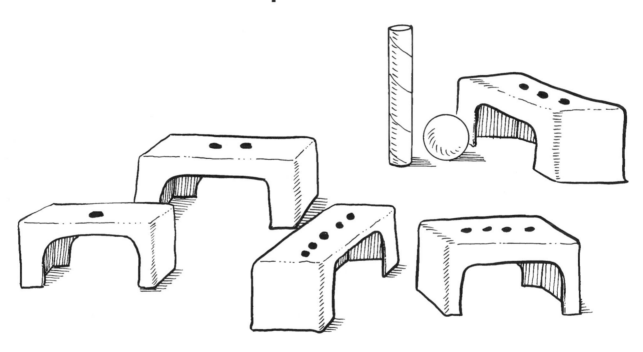

Materials

fifteen stick-on dots   five shoe boxes
paper towel tube   sponge ball

Activity

Make a set of croquet tunnels by cutting wide arches in the long sides of the shoe boxes. Place one dot on top of the first box, two dots on top of the second box and so on. Arrange the boxes in any order on the floor. Encourage the children to use the paper towel tube to hit the ball through the boxes, beginning with the box with one dot and moving through the others in order.

Kites

Materials

five construction paper kites with rope tails

Activity

Tie one knot in the tail of the first kite, two knots in the tail of the second kite and so on. Invite children to arrange the kites in order of least to most knots.
Note: Save the kites for activities in Chapter 7.

Any Time Ideas

◆ Reinforce order vocabulary with all classroom activities. In the block center, you might call attention to the tallest tower. When playing with playdough, you might notice the shortest snake or the largest ball.

◆ Ask children for ideas for arranging things in the classroom like papers to go home or puzzles or games on the shelf.

Suggestions for Home Involvement

◆ Give children yarn to take home. Ask them to cut a piece of yarn to match the height of each family member. They can use a piece of masking tape to identify which piece of yarn represents which person. When the children return, have them order the pieces of yarn from longest to shortest.

◆ Send home a copy of Home Connections on page 155.

Observations and Evaluations

◆ Arrange a group of objects in a specific order, such as largest to smallest or longest to shortest. Ask children to identify the order. If children cannot accomplish this, repeat Activities 2-12.

◆ Provide materials and ask children to create a variety of arrangements, such as tallest to shortest, biggest to smallest, heaviest to lightest and so on. Continue until all arrangements are covered. If children cannot accomplish this, repeat Activities 2-27.

◆ Give children three sets of buttons or counters. One set should include three members, one set six members and the last set nine members. Ask children to arrange the sets from the least members to the most members. If children cannot accomplish this, repeat Activities 31-40.

Resources

Children's Books

Allen, Pamela. *Who Sank the Boat?* Putnam, 1996.
Brett, Jan. *Goldilocks and the Three Bears.* Putnam, 1989.
Carle, Eric. *The Very Hungry Caterpillar.* Putnam, 1994.
Hoban, Tana. *Is It Larger? Is It Smaller?* Greenwillow, 1985.
Kalan, Robert. *Blue Sea.* Greenwillow, 1979.
Myller, Rolf. *How Big Is a Foot?* Dell, 1991.
Sendak, Maurice. *One Was Johnny.* Harper, 1962.
"The Little Red Hen." Many versions available.
"Three Billy Goats Gruff." Many versions available.

Records and Songs

Lucky, Sharron. "The Farmer in the Dell." *Sing Along with Lucky.* Melody House.
"Peanut Butter." *Where Is Thumbkin?* Kimbo.
"Twelve Days of Christmas."
"Here We Go 'Round the Mulberry Bush."

Home Connections

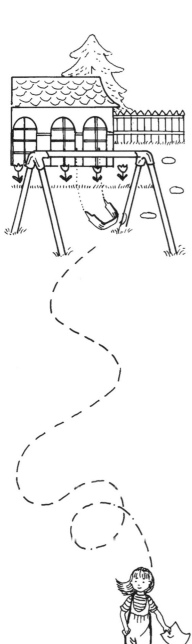

What's New? Ordering!

◆ The children are learning to put things in order. They are organizing and arranging objects and sets of objects by using one-to-one correspondence and sometimes by seeing that some sets have more or fewer members than others.

◆ Ordering will help your child understand that numbers have a specific order (fewer to more) and that each number is one more than the number before.

Fun and Easy Things You Can Do at Home

◆ Give your child nesting objects, like measuring cups and spoons, to play with.

◆ Talk about family order. Who is tall, taller, tallest? Who is shortest? Who is oldest? Who is youngest?

◆ Encourage your child to put food cans or boxes in order from smallest to biggest or lightest to heaviest.

◆ Encourage your child to help sort laundry items according to size (wash cloths, hand towels, bath towels, etc.).

Vocabulary Builders

These are some of our vocabulary words. Use them at home whenever you can.

big/bigger/biggest   first/next/last
heavy/heavier/heaviest   light/lighter/lightest
long/longer/longest   small/medium/large
short/shorter/shortest   tall/taller/tallest
top/middle/bottom

Book Corner

Next time you visit the library, check out one of these books:
Allen, Pamela. *Who Sank the Boat?* Putnam, 1996.
Hoban, Tana. *Is It Larger? Is It Smaller?* Greenwillow, 1985.
Kalan, Robert. *Blue Sea.* Greenwillow, 1979.
Myller, Rolf. *How Big Is a Foot?* Dell, 1991.

This page may be copied and sent home to parents.

Chapter 7

Numeration 1-5, Plus 0

Definition

Numeration is discovering and understanding the "manyness" of numbers. In this chapter, children will develop an understanding of the "manyness" of the numbers one through five. They will explore number families, learn to recognize numerals for each number and practice simple operations. Understanding that a set remains the same no matter what its configuration is an important part of children's conceptual understanding of number value. Addition is the union of sets. Subtraction is the inverse of addition, or the taking apart of sets.

Bridge to Other Math Concepts

Children generally understand the concept of one. They have been asking for "one" since learning to speak. The same is true for the number two, which has been part of children's knowledge bank since discovering they have two hands to hold whatever it is they want and realizing that two is one more than one. This chapter begins with presenting the number three. As each new number is introduced, it is presented as one more than the previous number. A major emphasis is placed on the set combinations for each number. The numeral that represents the number is introduced only after plenty of practice with set combinations. Zero is introduced at the end of the chapter.

Try the following activity before you begin this chapter. It will help children review concepts introduced in previous chapters, and it will allow you to check children's understanding.

◆ Give each child a handful of candy. Be sure each child has three kinds of candy.
◆ Ask children to describe the candies. List all the attributes they name.
◆ Instruct children to move their candies into several directional and positional relationships (in a pile, behind you, over your head, to one side, etc.).
◆ Ask the children to classify their candies and then explain their criteria.
◆ Have the children create a pattern with their candies.
◆ Instruct the children to classify their candies into sets and match them one to one.
◆ Ask the children to order their sets from least members to most members. Now you're ready for numeration.

Suggestions for Success

◆ Do not confuse children's ability to perform rote counting with their understanding of numbers.

◆ Since children's understanding of numbers is linked to their ability to conserve (recognize that a set doesn't change when it's configuration changes), this is a good time to reinforce activities that provide practice with conservation (playing with playdough, water, sand, etc.).

◆ Go through Activities 1-39 in this chapter focusing on the number three. Then repeat all activities focusing on the numbers four and five.

◆ As you introduce each number, introduce it as the adding of one more to the number the children just learned about. For example, when you introduce four, say, "We know what three is. When we add a new member to a set of three, we've created a set of four."

◆ Introduce zero after children demonstrate an understanding of numbers one through five. Zero is often a more difficult concept than the concept of nothing ("I have no candies" is easier to understand than "I have zero candies.").

◆ After you complete Activities 1-39 with numbers three through five and introduce zero in Activities 40-43, go on to Activities 44-54. These last activities allow children to demonstrate their knowledge of numbers one through five and zero.

◆ Add to number games as numbers are introduced. If you have a number/numeral matching game, don't add the number/numeral five until you've introduced it.

◆ Try to limit counting activities, other than songs, rhymes and stories, until children have studied numbers. This will encourage children to rely more on conceptual understanding and less on rote memorization.

Key Words

adding on	addition	counting on	empty set
equals	five	four	member
minus	none	number	number family
numeral	one	plus	set
subtraction	sum	symbol	three
two	zero		

Circle Time Story: Counting Clover Leaves

1

Materials

real clover leaves, if available, if not use construction paper clover leaf cutouts (3 leaves)

Heather was in the backyard looking for four leaf clovers. She had heard her older sister Jill talking about how lucky four leaf clovers were and she really wanted to find one. Heather had gathered a handful of clovers. She went inside to ask her mother if any of the clovers she had picked had four leaves.

Heather didn't know how to count. She waited patiently as her mother looked at each clover. When her mother was finished looking she said, "I'm sorry, Heather, but all of these are three leaf clovers."

"How can you tell?" asked Heather.
"By counting," said her mother. "I counted the leaves on each of the clovers."

"Show me," said Heather.

"Okay. You know how to count to two, don't you?" Heather nodded yes. "Show me with your hands," her mother said. Heather held up two hands.

"That's right. Now three is one more than two. Let's look at one of these clovers."

Heather's mother pulled a leaf from one of the clovers and placed it in one of Heather's hands. Then she pulled another leaf from the clover and placed it in Heather's other hand. "Now," Heather's mother said, "how many leaves are left?"

"Only one," said Heather. "Three is one more than two. Now I know how to recognize a clover with three leaves. How will I know when I find a clover with four leaves?"

"Four is one more than three," answered her mother.

"Okay," said Heather. And she ran outside to look again.

Materials for Story Extension

construction paper cutouts of a three leaf clover
drawing paper
crayons

Activity

Encourage the children to make crayon rubbings of the clovers. If real clovers are available, go on a clover hunt.

2   Making a Set

Materials

stringing beads
books
crayons

Activity

Have two children stand. Ask the other children how many are in the set. When they answer two, ask how many more children need to stand to make a set of three. Have children try this activity using stringing beads. Encourage them to string two beads, then ask how many more beads they need to make a set of three. When they answer one, repeat the activity using books and crayons.

3

Three Sets of Three

Materials

three carpet squares, mats or towels

Activity

Divide the class into three groups. Lay out three carpet squares. Ask one child from each group to stand on one of the carpet squares. When children are in place, ask a second child from each group to join the first child on the carpet square. Ask the children how many children are on each carpet square. After they identify each set as two, ask them how many more children need to go to each carpet square to make a set of three.

 NUMBER FAMILIES

ACTIVITIES **4** TO **15**

 4

Number Bags

Materials

ziplock bags (one per child)
small counters (washers, pennies, buttons, etc.)
permanent marker

Activity

Put three counters inside each ziplock bag and seal it. Use a permanent marker to make a vertical line down the middle of each bag from the top (sealed part) to the bottom. Show children how to move the counters on either side of the line to create set combinations. Allow enough practice for children to internalize the concept that three is three no matter what the combination or configuration of its members.

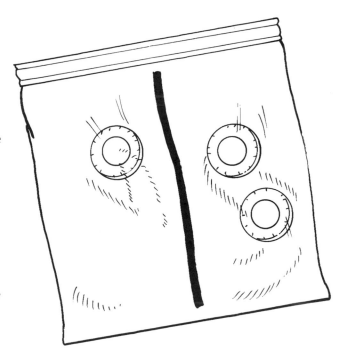

5   Children Combinations

Materials

masking tape, rope or yarn

Activity

Place a strip of masking tape, rope or yarn on the floor. Ask three children to stand on one side of the tape. Ask the other children how many children are in the set. When they state that there are three children, move one of the children to the other side of the masking tape line. Ask the children if the set is still three. Explain that there are many ways to arrange the set and that it is still three. Demonstrate the set combinations of three.

6   Recording Combinations

Materials

sheet of drawing paper for each child
1″ construction paper squares
glue

Activity

Give each child a sheet of drawing paper that has been folded down the middle. Provide colored squares and glue so they can create one of the examples from the set combinations for three that they identified when using their number bags. Encourage the children to describe their example.

7   Sweet Sets

Materials

two kinds of candy

Activity

Place two kinds of candy in a bowl. Have children take three candies from the bowl and create a set combination (two peppermints and one butterscotch make a set of three candies, three peppermints make a set of three, etc.).

8 Drop a Set

Materials

paper plate
counters

Activity

Draw a line down the middle of a paper plate. Have children drop three counters on the plate. Ask them to describe the set combination they have created.

9 Drop a Set II

Materials

3/4" washers (spray paint one side to make two-sided counters)
carpet squares

Activity

Give the children three washers (two-sided counters) and encourage them to drop them onto a carpet square. Ask them to describe the set combinations that result from the two colors.

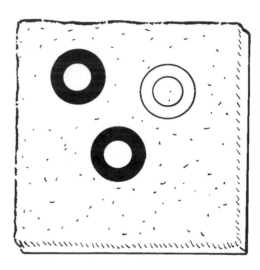

10 Guess a Set

Materials

3/4" washers (spray paint one side)
box

Activity

Invite the children to guess which set combination will be formed when you drop three washers into the box. Drop the washers. Let the children look in the box to see if their guess is correct.

11 Changing Directions

Materials

three carpet squares or three sheets of construction paper

Activity

Place the carpet squares or sheets of construction paper in a horizontal line on the floor. Ask the children how many carpet squares are in the set. After they identify the carpet squares as a set of three, rearrange the squares into a vertical line and ask the question again. Continue the activity using as many different configurations as possible.

12 Mine's Different

Materials

buttons

Activity

Place children in small groups. Ask each group to sit in a circle. Give each child a set of three buttons. Ask a child to make a set combination with the buttons and describe it. Then let the next child make a set combination. Continue around the circle.

13 Visual Sets

Materials

three pennies or three counters
paper
overhead projector

Activity

Place pennies or counters on the overhead in a set of one, two or three. Turn the overhead on and off quickly and ask the children to identify the set they saw. Change the set and continue the activity.

14 Conservation

Materials

six pennies or six counters
overhead projector

Activity

Place counters on the overhead in two horizontal lines with three counters in each line. Put the counters close together in one line and spread them out in the other. Ask the children if there are the same number of counters in each line. Ask them to count the counters in each line. Continue, using several other configurations of three.

15 Dot Families

Materials

two colors of 1″ stick-on dots

Activity

Give the children the two colors of stick-on dots and encourage them to create set combinations for the number three.

 INTRODUCING NUMERALS

ACTIVITIES 16 TO 24

16 Tally Marks

Materials

paper
crayons
number bags

Activity

Give children the number bags for the number three (see Activity 4). Encourage them to use tally marks to record the set combinations they create.

17 Symbol

Materials

index card for
  each child
counters
ink pads

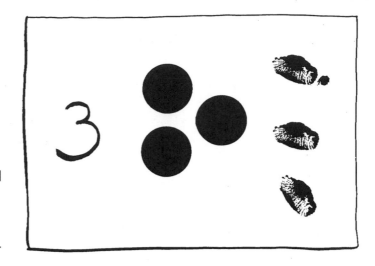

Activity

Draw the numeral 3 on the index cards and give them to the children. Ask the children to place three counters on their cards. Explain that the symbol on the card represents three. Let the children use the ink pad to make fingerprints on the index card.

18 Playdough Numerals

Materials

playdough

Activity

Give the children playdough and encourage them to make the numeral 3.

19 Grainy Numerals

Materials

salt or sand
cookie sheet or shallow box

Activity

Fill a cookie sheet or shallow box with sand or salt and have the children draw numerals with their fingers.

20   Numeral Rubbings

Materials
sandpaper
drawing paper
crayons

Activity
Cut numerals out of sandpaper and allow children to make crayon rubbings of them.

21   Tactile Numerals

Materials
glue
paper

Activity
Write the numeral 3 on a piece of paper for each child or, if children are able, encourage them to write the numeral themselves. Provide a bottle of glue and invite children to make glue drops on top of the numeral. Allow the glue to dry. Encourage children to trace over the numeral with their fingers and feel the raised effect of the glue.

22   Numeral Hunt

Materials
none

Activity
Encourage children to go on a numeral hunt to find classroom items that have the numeral 1, 2 or 3 on them (clock, calendar, book pages, games).

23   Egg Carton Shake

Materials

egg carton
button
small pictures of a dog, a cat and a bird

Activity

Write the numerals 1, 2 and 3 three times each in the sections of an egg carton.
Paste a picture of a dog in one of the remaining sections, a cat in another and a
bird in the last. Invite children to place a button in the egg carton, close the lid and
shake. Then ask the children to open the lid and see where the button has landed.
If it is on a numeral, have the children name the numeral. If it is on one of the
animals, have the children make that animal's sound (cat meows, dog barks, bird
whistles song).

24   Numeral Toss

Materials

shower curtain or butcher paper
permanent marker
beanbags

Activity

Place the shower curtain or butcher paper on the floor and write the numerals 1,
2 and 3 on it. Invite children to call out a numeral and then toss the beanbag on
top of that numeral.

25 Why Count?

Materials

chart paper
marker

Activity

Encourage children to list the reasons why knowing how to count is important (to find out how much money we have, how many candles are on a cake, how many leaves are on a clover, etc.). List their ideas on the chart paper. Leave the list up and add to it as children discover more reasons.

26 Counting Children

Materials

Activity

Ask three children to stand. Let the rest of the children help you count the standing children. Demonstrate that no matter where the children are standing in relationship to each other, they are still a set of three. Be sure all children understand that it takes all three children to make a set of three (not just the child in the third position).

27 Snack Counters

Materials

napkins
crackers

Activity

Place a napkin for each child on the snack table. Provide a box of crackers and ask each child to count three crackers onto his or her napkin.

28 Carpet Count

Materials

three carpet squares

Activity

Place the carpet squares a few inches apart on the floor. Ask the children to walk across the squares, counting each square as they go. Watch for counting errors, such as counting a square twice or skipping a square. Try the activity again, letting the children hop across the squares.

29 Numbers on a Rope (number line)

Materials

clothesline rope
construction paper
marker
hole punch

Activity

Write the word Start and the numerals 1, 2 and 3 on sheets of construction paper and laminate them. Punch two holes in each sheet of paper and thread the clothesline through it. (Be sure to leave room on the rope to add numerals. You will add 4, 5 and 0 in this chapter and 6-10 in Chapter 9.) Place the rope on the floor and ask the children to stand on Start (Start will be replaced with 0 later). Ask the children to take three steps along the number line and then check to see if they are standing on the numeral 3. Review 1 and 2 as well.

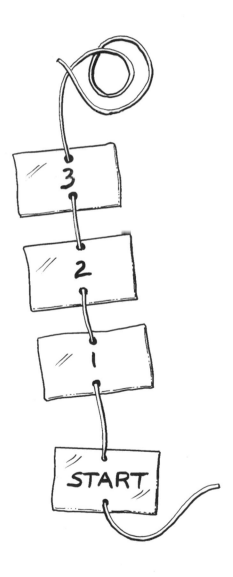

30

I Can Count

Materials
numeral cards with the numerals 1, 2 and 3
paper clips

Activity
Encourage children to count the correct number of paper clips for each numeral card and then clip the paper clips to the cards.

 31

Number Books

Materials
ziplock bags
poster board cut to fit inside the bags
colored plastic tape
crayons

Activity
Make a number baggie book by stapling the ziplock bags together across the bottom (the "unzippered" side) and placing a piece of tape over the staples. Write the numerals 1, 2 and 3 on separate pieces of poster board. Let the children draw the corresponding number of objects on each one. Insert the poster board pieces into the bags. (Repeat when learning 4 and 5 and save for activities in Chapter 9.)

32 Number Plates

Materials
three paper plates
buttons or other counters

Activity
Write one each of the numerals 1, 2 and 3 on three paper plates. Invite children to count the correct number of buttons or counters onto each plate.

33 Animal Count

Materials
berry baskets
plastic animals
index cards and marker

Activity
Use the berry baskets as animal cages. Assign each cage a numeral. Encourage the children to count then place the correct number of animals into each cage.

34 Singing Number Songs

Materials

Activity

Sing as many songs as the children can think of that mention the numbers one to three, for example, "Three Little Monkeys Jumping on the Bed" and "Baa Baa, Black Sheep." You can change the word five to three in other songs, such as "Five White Ducks" and "Five Little Speckled Frogs."

35 Classroom Sets

Materials

yarn
scissors

Activity

Make enough large yarn circles on the floor to accommodate all the children when they are grouped by threes. Invite one child at a time to choose a circle and stand inside it. Continue until all the children have chosen a circle. Once a circle contains three members, consider it full and encourage the children to choose another circle.

36 Bell Bags

Materials

three 4"x 8" pieces of felt
three 1" strips of Velcro
six jingle bells
appliqué numerals 1, 2 and 3
glue

Activity

Fold the pieces of felt in half and hot glue two sides to form a bag. Glue the numeral 1 on one bag, 2 on another and 3 on the last. Glue a 1" strip of Velcro at the top of each bag to form a clasp. Put one bell in the bag with the numeral 1 on it, two bells in the bag with the numeral 2 and three bells in the bag with the numeral 3. Allow children to explore the bags, putting them in numerical order and in order of lightest to heaviest and softest sound to loudest sound.

37 Peanut Count

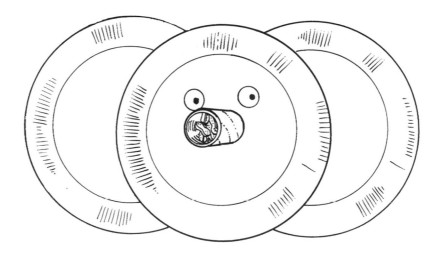

Materials

three paper plates
paintbrush
glue
peanuts in the shell, optional

gray paint
empty toilet paper tube
wiggly eyes, crayons or markers

Activity

Paint the three paper plates and the toilet paper tube gray. Stand the tube in the center of one plate and glue it. This makes an elephant's head and trunk. Glue the other two plates to the first plate to make the elephant's ears. Glue on wiggly eyes or draw eyes with a marker. Invite the children to drop and count peanuts into the elephant's trunk. Later, they can enjoy the peanuts during snack time.

38

Baggie Fish

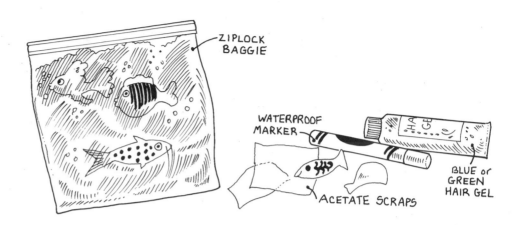

ZIPLOCK BAGGIE

WATERPROOF MARKER

BLUE or GREEN HAIR GEL

ACETATE SCRAPS

Materials

scissors
waterproof marking pens
measuring cup

acetate (scraps of laminating film work great)
ziplock bag for each child
green or blue hair gel

Activity

Cut fish shapes from the acetate. Let children take three fish and color them with the markers. Have children scoop 1 cup of hair gel into their ziplock bag and then place their three fish inside the bag. Make sure bags are securely closed.

 39

Ordinal Numbers

Materials

three carpet squares or three sheets of construction paper

Activity

Place the carpet squares on the floor. Encourage the children to walk across the squares as they count (as they did in Activity 28). This time ask the children to identify where they stepped first, next and last. Have the children do this activity again identifying the positions as first, second and third. With older children, play a modified form of baseball and identify the bases as first, second and third.

40   The Empty Set

Materials

Activity

Teach the children the song "Five Little Ducks."

Five little ducks went out to play. (hold up five fingers)
Over the hill and far away. (hold hand above eyes as if looking far away)
Mama Duck called with a "Quack! Quack! Quack!" (clap hands on quacks)
Four little ducks came swimming back. (hold up four fingers)

Four little ducks went out to play.
Over the hill and far away. . . .

Continue until no little ducks come swimming back. After performing the hand motions with the whole group, select five children to be the five little ducks and act out the song for the rest of the class. Make arrangements for the ducks to actually disappear, perhaps behind a bookshelf or divider. When all the ducks are gone and "no little ducks came swimming back," ask the children to tell you how many ducks are left. When the children say "none," explain that we have a number and a name for a set that has nothing in it. Tell them that a set with no members is called the empty set. The number for the empty set is zero. You may want to practice this with duck cutouts or flannel board pieces. You can demonstrate the empty set with other counting songs and fingerplays that count backwards.

41   More Practice with the Empty Set

Materials

three counters
sheet of paper

Activity

Lay three counters on the floor and cover them with a sheet of paper. Uncover them and ask children to tell you how many counters are in the set. Remove one counter and repeat the process. Continue until you have no counters. Ask children to tell you how many counters are in the set.

42 Symbol for Zero

Materials
see Activities 18, 19, 20 and 21

Activity
Repeat Activities 18, 19, 20 and 21 using the numeral 0.

43 Adding Zero to the Number Line

Materials
number line rope from Activity 29
construction paper
marker

Activity
Write the numeral 0 on a sheet of construction paper and laminate it. Punch two holes in the paper. Replace the Start card on your number rope with this card.

Simple Operations

The next ten activities deal with addition and subtraction.

◆ Do these activities after children have mastered Activities 1-43. Some children may not be ready to move beyond this point and will do better to continue constructing their understanding of previously introduced concepts.
◆ With children who are ready, introduce the symbols for plus (+), minus (-) and equals (=) before starting Activities 44-54.
◆ Keep in mind that anytime children manipulate materials for addition or subtraction, they need to describe their actions. Model and encourage the use of number sentences. For example, "Two marbles plus three marbles equals five marbles."
◆ Keep in mind that anytime children use either addition or subtraction they should check their work using the inverse (opposite) operation. For example, "Two marbles plus three marbles equals five marbles. Five marbles minus three marbles equals two marbles."

44 Feely Box Numbers

Materials

five counters

Activity

Divide children into groups of three. Place five counters in a feely box. Invite one child (Player 1) to reach in the feely box and take some of the counters out. Ask another child (Player 2) to reach into the box and take out more counters. Player 1 gives counters to Player 3, calling out the number of counters. Player 3 says "and," signaling Player 2 to hand over counters and call out their number. Player 3 says "equals" and calls out the total number of counters in hand. For example

Player 1 draws two counters from the feely box.
Player 2 draws three counters.
Player 1 says "two" and places counters in Player 3's hand.
Player 3 says "and" and turns to Player 2.
Player 2 says "three" and places counters in Player 3's hand.
Player 3 says "equals five."

45 Equation Boards

Materials

cardboard
   (approximately 8" x 11")
elastic string
beads

Activity

Write + and = signs on the cardboard. String beads on the elastic, then tie it around the board. Encourage children to move the beads along the elastic to illustrate number sentences as they say them.

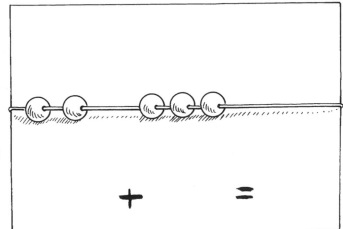

46   Addition Sacks

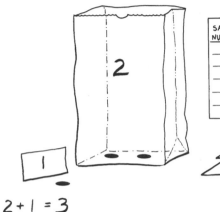

$2 + 1 = 3$

Materials

six paper sacks   index cards
markers   counters

Activity

Write the numerals 0-5 on the sacks. Make numeral cards for each sack by writing the numerals shown in the chart on index cards. Stack each set of cards in front of the appropriate sack and place the number of counters shown in the chart inside the sack. Invite children to draw a card, add the number of counters shown on the card to those in the sack and state the total number of counters. The number of counters in the sack will validate their answers. Encourage children to say a number sentence that explains what they've done.

---

47   Slide the Sum

Materials

poster board
three colored-paper squares
objects

Activity

Glue the colored paper squares onto the poster board to serve as place holders in number sentences (see illustration). Place a set of objects in each square. As you say the sentence, slide all the objects across the equal sign.

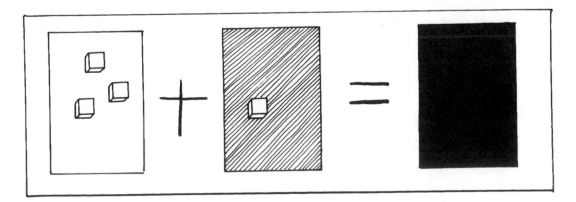

48

Paper Clip Addition

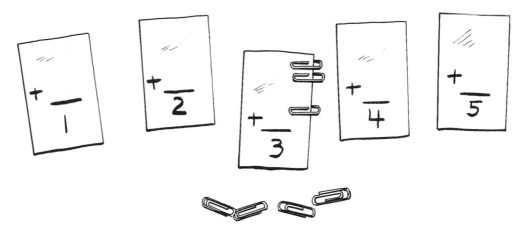

Materials

index cards
contact paper or laminating machine
paper clips
crayon, optional

Activity

Write number sentences on five index cards. Include the + symbol and the
sum (1-5) but not the addends. Laminate the cards. Encourage the children to use
paper clips on the cards to fill in the blanks of the sentences. Children can also
write in the missing addends with a crayon and wipe it off later.

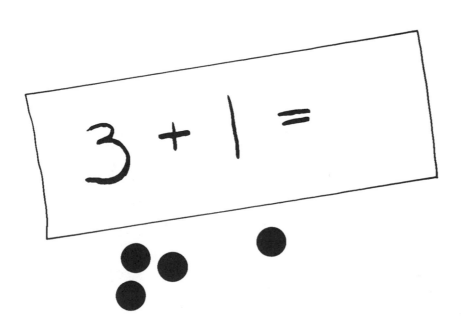

49

Symbolic Representation

Materials

poster board
marker
counters

Activity

Write number sentences on
strips of poster board. Invite
children to use counters to
figure out the answers. (Be sure
to write sentences horizontally
and vertically.)

50 Subtraction Sacks

Materials

six paper sacks   index cards
markers   counters

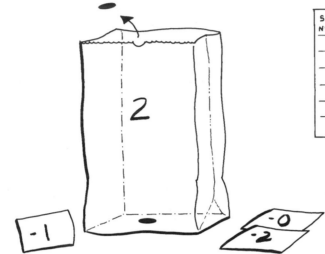

$2 - 1 = 1$

SACK NUMBER	NUMBER OF COUNTERS	NUMERAL CARDS
0	0	-0
1	1	-0, -1
2	2	-0, -1, -2
3	3	-0, -1, -2, -3
4	4	-0, -1, -2, -3, -4
5	5	-0, -1, -2, -3, -4, -5

Activity

Write the numerals 0-5 on the sacks. Make numeral cards for each sack by writing the numerals shown in the chart on index cards. Stack each set of cards in front of the appropriate sack and place the number of counters shown in the chart inside the sack. Invite children to draw a card, subtract the number of counters shown on the card from the sack and state the number of counters that are left. The number of counters in the sack will validate their answer. Encourage children to say a number sentence that explains what they've done.

51 Clothespin Drop

Materials

five clothespins
wide-mouth jar

Activity

Invite each child to start with five clothespins. Encourage them to try dropping the clothespins into the jar. Use the clothespins inside and outside the jar to make up number sentences. For example, if two clothespins land outside the jar and three land inside the jar, say "Five minus two equals three" or "You started with five clothespins, two are in the jar. How many are left on the floor?"

52 Drop a Hanky

Materials

counters
paper plate
facial tissue

Activity

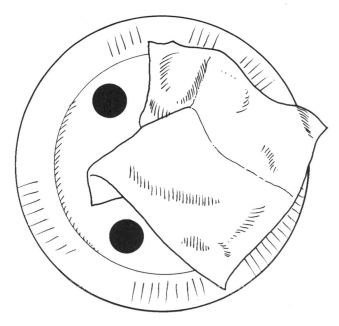

Place up to five counters on a paper plate, then invite a child to drop the tissue over them. Use the covered and uncovered counters to create number sentences. For example, you started with five counters on the plate and the tissue covers four of them. Say "Five minus four equals one." You can also do this activity with an overhead projector. Use a sheet of paper to cover counters.

53 Tower Equations

Materials

multilink or unifix cubes

Activity

Encourage children to build towers of two to five cubes. Break the tower, then use the pieces to construct a number sentence. For example, break a tower of five cubes into one set of two and one set of three to demonstrate five minus two equals three.

Hide It Under a Basket

Materials

five balls, blocks or other material
basket or box

Activity

Give two players a set of two to five balls, blocks or any other material. Cover Player 1's eyes while Player 2 hides some of the objects in a basket or box. Encourage Player 1 to count the number of objects showing and figure out how many objects are hidden. Have the players create a number sentence to explain the problem. For example, Megin had five balls, now she has two. How many are hidden?

Any Time Ideas

◆ Show children the numerals on book pages (up to the numeral children are familiar with).
◆ Use counting to three as a means of starting an activity or getting children to do something in unison.
◆ Perform fingerplays or sing songs that focus on three such as "Three Little Monkeys Jumping on the Bed."
◆ Give children a choice of three learning centers.

Suggestions for Home Involvement

◆ Give children a bag and ask them to bring a set of three objects from home. Let them display their items for others to view.
◆ Send home a copy of Home Connections on page 184.

Observations and Evaluations

◆ Display sets of objects with one to five members. Ask children to count the members of each set. Provide numeral cards for numbers one to five. Ask children to match the appropriate numeral card to each set. If children cannot accomplish this, repeat Activities 25-38.
◆ Give children sets of three, four and five objects. Have them demonstrate set combinations for each set of objects. If children cannot accomplish this, repeat Activities 2-15.
◆ Ask children to demonstrate counting the items in a set with three members. After they have counted, ask them to show you three. If they hand you the set, it indicates they have a conceptual understanding of three. If they hand you the item in the third position, repeat Activities 2-15. Do the same activity for four and five.

Resources

Children's Books

Aker, Suzanne. *What Comes in Twos, Threes, and Fours?* Simon & Schuster, 1990.

Allen, Jonathan. *One With a Bun.* Morrow, 1992.

Anno, Mitsumasa. *Anno's Counting Book.* HarperCollins, 1977.

Beck, Ian. *Five Little Ducks.* Holt, 1993.

Bennett, David. *One Cow, Moo, Moo!* Holt, 1990.

Bishop, Claire. *Five Chinese Brothers.* Putnam, 1989.

Carle, Eric. *1, 2, 3 to the Zoo.* Putnam, 1996.

Christelow, Eileen. *Five Little Monkeys Jumping on the Bed.* Clarion, 1989.

_____. Five Little *Monkeys Sitting in a Tree.* Houghton Mifflin, 1991.

Fleming, Denise. *Count!* Holt, 1992.

Geringer, Laura. *A Three Hat Day.* HarperCollins, 1987.

Hong, Lily Toy. *Two of Everything.* Albert Whitman, 1993.

Moncure, Jane. *My One Book.* Child's World, 1985.

Raffi. *Five Little Ducks.* Crown, 1989.

"The Three Bears." Many versions available.

"Three Billy Goats Gruff." Many versions available.

"Three Little Pigs." Many versions available.

West, Colin. *One Little Elephant.* Candlewick, 1994.

Ziefert, Harriet. *The Three Wishes.* Puffin, 1993.

Records and Songs

Gunsberg, Andrew. "Pumpkins One Two Three." *Saddle Up Your Pony.* Folkways.

Jenkins, Ella. "A German Counting Rhyme." *Hopping Around from Place to Place.* Educational Activities.

Millang, Steve and Greg Scelsa. "1, 2, Buckle My Shoe." *We All Live Together, Volume 3.* Youngheart.

Sharon, Lois and Bram. "Once I Saw Three Goats." *Singing 'n Swinging.* Elephant.

____. "Three Little Monkeys." *Smorgasbord.* Elephant.

Scruggs, Joe. "Crocodile Song." *Deep in the Jungle.* Shadow Play.

"Five Little Speckled Frogs."

"Five Little Ducks."

"One Elephant," "Five Little Ducks," "Three Little Monkeys," and "Five Fat Turkeys." *Where Is Thumbkin?* Kimbo.

Home Connections

What's New?   Numeration 1-5 and 0!

We are learning about and working with the numbers zero through five. Soon we will be able to count to five, recognize numerals 0-5 and perform simple addition and subtraction operations.

Fun and Easy Things You Can Do at Home

◆ Encourage your child to count things like dinner plates and glasses (up to five).
◆ Point out numerals in everyday life. Look at phone numbers, addresses, license plates and other things with numerals.
◆ Look through family pictures. Show your child pictures from when he or she was one, two, three, four and five years old.

Vocabulary Builders

These are some of our vocabulary words. Use them at home whenever you can.

adding on	addition
counting on	equals
minus	number
number family	numeral
plus	subtraction
zero/one/two/three/four/five	

Book Corner

Next time you visit the library, check out one of these books:
Anno, Mitsumasa. *Anno's Counting Book*. HarperCollins, 1977.
Christelow, Eileen. *Five Little Monkeys Jumping on the Bed*. Clarion, 1989.
Geringer, Laura. *A Three Hat Day*. HarperCollins, 1987.
Gray, Catherine. *One, Two, Three, and Four, No More?* Houghton Mifflin, 1988.
Moncure, Jane. *My One Book*. Child's World, 1985.
Raffi. *Five Little Ducks*. Crown, 1989.

This page may be copied and sent home to parents.

Chapter 8

Shapes

Definition

Children learn about shapes by recognizing geometric figures and distinguishing the similarities and differences of their attributes.

Bridge to Other Math Concepts

Children need to have a conceptual understanding of the numbers three and four before they can understand the specific number of sides and corners that are the distinctive attributes of geometric shapes. They also need an understanding of long and short and their variations, which were studied in Chapter 5, in order to see the difference between a rectangle and a square. The ability to identify shapes lays a foundation for understanding the principles of geometry.

Suggestions for Success

◆ Use the terminology ___ sides and ___ corners when introducing each shape. This helps solidify the distinctive differences in attributes. For example, describe a circle as having no sides and no corners, a square as having four sides and four corners and so on.
◆ Be aware that, by definition (number of sides and corners), a rectangle and a square have the same number of sides and corners. The lengths of the sides makes the square a specific kind of rectangle.
◆ Use straws to form and introduce the shapes that have corners and sides.

Key Words

circle	corner
closed	curved
oval	rectangle
round	side
square	straight
triangle	

1

Circle Time Story:
Silly Circle's Big Escape

Materials

poster board circle (approximately 12" in diameter) with a happy face drawn on it
chalk and chalkboard
Note: Use chalk to make designs on the chalkboard as Silly makes them in the story. You can tell this story all in one setting to introduce shapes in general, or you can tell the story in segments and introduce specific shapes one at a time.

Silly Circle loved her place in Ms. Bryant's classroom. She sat on the chalkboard rail with the other shapes, Terrific Triangle, Ready Rectangle and Super Square. Ms. Bryant drew a beautiful smiling face on Silly Circle and every day the children would talk about her, describe her round shape and play games where they would roll her across the floor. Silly Circle was a great roller. She had no sides and no corners.

While the children played, Silly Circle heard them talk about all the wonderful things they did when they left school each day. She longed to see the park the children talked about and, especially, she longed to see the place they called "my backyard." She wanted to see the garden Kathy said grew in her backyard and the swimming pool John said was in his backyard.

One day a strange and exciting thing happened. Ms. Bryant let the children take the shapes outside during play time. The children were taking turns rolling Silly Circle back and forth to each other. When it was John's turn to roll Silly Circle, he pushed her so hard that she rolled right through the open space in the gate and down the sidewalk, across the street and into an open field. It all happened so fast, Silly Circle hardly knew what to think. She looked around and saw that she was on her own.

Silly Circle took a deep breath and decided this was her opportunity to see the world. She began to roll. She rolled past stores, cars, houses, animals . . . all the things the children talked about. Soon she came to a green grassy area with lots of trees. She looked up and read the sign at the gate. It said Millstown Park. "This is it," thought Silly Circle, and she rolled right through the gate.

Inside, Silly saw a large sandy area with a tall slide, swings and a merry-go-round. She rolled over to take a closer look. Silly noticed she was leaving a trail in the sand. "Wow," she thought. "This is just like writing."

She rolled from the slide to the swings and from the swings to the merry-go-round. Silly looked at the design that she had drawn in the sand. "Mmm," she said. "Three sides and three corners. I made a triangle. It looks just like my friend Terrific."

Silly decided to leave the park and roll over to the houses across the street. She rolled around one of the houses and saw what had to be a swimming pool. It was just like what John had described. It was shaped like her friend Ready Rectangle. It had four sides and four corners. Two of its sides were long and two were short. Silly rolled through some water that had been splashed out of the pool and immediately saw she could write again. "I'm going to check this out," thought Silly.

She began to roll around the pool counting the sides as she rolled. One - two - three - four sides and, as she looked at the water line she had drawn around the pool, she saw there were one, two, three, four corners, too.

Just then Silly looked up and saw a vegetable garden in the yard next door. She rolled through a tiny space in the fence and went to investigate the garden. She rolled across the first row and then down the side and across the back row and up the last side.

"This is a square garden," thought Silly. "Four equal sides, just like my friend Super." She saw that once again she had left a trail in the dirt. She looked at what she had drawn, four equal sides and four corners. Seeing the square shape somehow made Silly lonesome. She missed her friends.

Silly started back the way she had come. She saw the garden, the pool, the park and the field outside the school where she had started her journey. She rolled around in a circle trying to remember which way she needed to go. Just then Silly heard children calling her name. She looked in the direction of the noise. Kathy and John were saying, "There's Silly Circle!"

Just then Silly felt a warm hand pick her up. It was Ms. Bryant.

"Silly Circle, I have been looking for you. The children were afraid you were lost," said Ms. Bryant.

Silly Circle loved all the things she had seen but she was really happy to be back home.

Materials for Story Extension
cookie sheet
sand or salt

Activity
Give the children the cookie sheet filled with sand or salt and encourage them to make the shapes like Silly did, using their fingers to draw. Draw the shapes on the chalkboard for them to copy.

2

Circle Games

Materials

Activity

Play circle games with the children such as "Duck, Duck, Goose" or "Dog and the Bone." Try circle dances such as "Hokey Pokey" or "Ring Around the Rosie." Ask the children to tell you what shape they are forming as they stand in their groups. Ask if there are any sides or corners.

 3

Circle, Circle

Materials

cardboard circle templates   jar lids
margarine tubs   paper
crayons

Activity

Encourage children to trace the circle templates to make designs on the paper.

 4

Paper Chains

Materials

3/4" strips of construction paper
glue

Activity

Show the children how to make paper chains. After they've each made one, join all the chains together and see how big a circle they make.

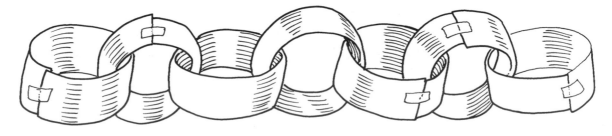

5   # Easel Circles

Materials
easel paper cut in circle shapes
paint and brushes

Activity
Place the cut-out circles at the easel and encourage the children to paint on them.

 6   # Tire Rolling

Materials
tires

Activity
Show the tires and encourage the children to describe them. Are they circles? Do the tires have sides or corners? Invite the children to have a tire rolling contest.

 7   # Water Painting

Materials
paintbrushes
buckets of water

Activity
Encourage the children to paint water circles on the sidewalk like Silly did.

 8   # Hula Hoop Fun

Materials
hula hoops

Activity
Show the hula hoops and ask, "Are they circles? Are there any sides or corners?" Have a contest to see who can keep the hula hoop going around his or her body the longest.

9 Make a Pizza Face

Materials

English muffins
pizza sauce
mozzarella cheese
pimientos
olives
plastic knives
toaster oven

Activity

Give each child an English muffin. Ask children to look at their muffin's shape and describe it. Encourage children to spread sauce on the muffin and put a piece of cheese on top. Provide sliced olives and pimientos so the children can make a face. Bake in a toaster oven.

 OVAL

10 Bendable Circles

Materials

pipe cleaners

Activity

Give the children pipe cleaners to fashion into ovals. Ask children if there are any sides or corners in their ovals.
Note: With young children, make an oval first with a pipe cleaner. Use the pipe cleaners to make other shapes.

11 Egg Rolling

Materials

hard boiled eggs
natural dyes—beet juice, tea, blueberry juice, optional
masking tape
golf balls

Activity

Ask children to bring a hard boiled egg from home. Make sure you bring some extras for those who forget. If appropriate, dye and decorate the eggs. Put two strips of masking tape about five feet apart on the floor. Invite the children to place an egg and a golf ball on one strip of tape and roll them to the other strip. What happens? How is the egg different from the golf ball?

 TRIANGLE

 12

Build a Triangle

Materials

straws cut in different
    lengths
playdough

Activity

Encourage children to make triangles with the straws and use the playdough to hold the corners together. Ask the children to describe their work in terms of numbers of sides and corners.

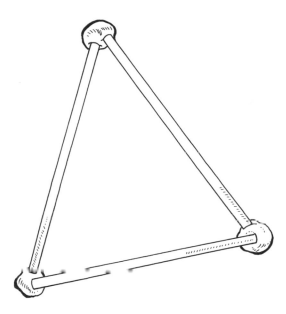

 13

Triangle Prints

Materials

sponges
scissors
tempera paint
paper

Activity

Cut the sponges into triangles. Allow the children to print designs on the paper using the triangular sponges.

14   Triangle Snacks

Materials
pretzel sticks
cheddar cheese cubes

Activity
Encourage the children to make triangles with the pretzel sticks and use the cheese to hold the corners together. Let the children eat their triangles.

15   Triangle Builders

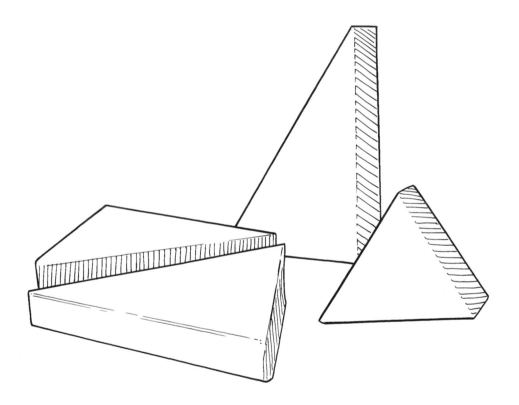

Materials
triangular-shaped blocks

Activity
Have children build structures in the block center using only the triangular blocks.

16 Easel Triangles

Materials

easel paper cut in triangular shapes
tempera paint
brushes

Activity

Encourage the children to paint on the triangular paper.

17 Triangle Music Makers

Materials

triangle from rhythm band instruments

Activity

Ask children to identify the shape of the triangle. Ask them to count the sides and corners. Encourage them to play the instrument.

18 Roll a Triangle

Materials

ball
yarn, optional

Activity

Place three children in position so that when a ball is rolled between them a triangle is formed. Make enough groups so that all children are included. Have the groups begin rolling the ball at the same time and see which group can go the longest without one of its members missing the ball. You can do a similar activity with a long piece of yarn tied together at the ends. Invite three children to hold the yarn and form a triangle with it.

19

Build a Rectangle

Materials

straws cut in two lengths
playdough

Activity

Encourage children to make rectangular shapes with the straws and use the playdough to hold the corners together. Ask children to describe their work in terms of numbers of sides and corners. Are the sides the same? Which sides are longer? Which sides are shorter?

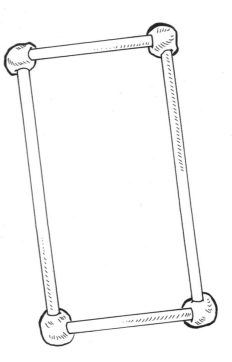

 20

Rectangle Hunt

Materials

Activity

Have the children look around the classroom for items shaped like a rectangle (tables, chalkboards, books, carpet squares, blocks, etc.).

 21

Rectangle Tracks

Materials

two shallow boxes, one 9″ x 12″ and one 8″ x 11″ or two boxes that have
   approximately the same size relationship
paper cut to the size of the larger box
marble
tempera paint

Activity

Lay the paper in the larger box and then place the smaller box on top, creating a 1/2" track around the edges. Dip the marble in the paint and place it in the track. Roll it around the track several times and then remove the marble. Take the boxes apart to see the rectangle that was formed.

 22

Rectangle Pairs

Materials

Activity

Ask the children to select a partner. How many ways can they put their bodies together to form a rectangle?

23

Human Rectangles

Materials

large rectangular boxes
scissors and tape

Activity

Cut the bottom out of a large rectangular box. Cut a half circle out of the other end to make a place for a head. Cut two holes for the arms. Encourage children to dress in the rectangle costumes and do a dance.

24

Build a Square

Materials

straws   playdough

Activity

Encourage children to make squares with the straws and use playdough to hold the corners together. Ask the children to describe their work in terms of sides and corners.

 25

Hopscotch

Materials

chalk   beanbag

Activity

Draw a hopscotch grid on the sidewalk and encourage children to play. Draw children's attention to the fact that the hopscotch game is made of squares.

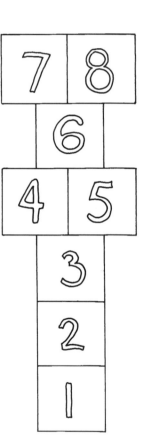

 26

Square Popsicles

Materials

juice or punch   ice tray

Activity

Pour the juice or punch into the ice tray. Freeze and serve the square popsicles.

27   **Square Dancing**

Materials

square dance music

Activity

Have children choose partners. Arrange children in square dance formations (four sets of partners in each square). Encourage children to perform these simple steps:

Bow to your partner.
Swing your partner. (lock arms and spin around twice)
Do-si-do. (fold arms across chest and "back" around your partner)
Promenade. (partners hold hands, right and left hands together,
   and walk around the square)

Ask children if they know why the dance is called Square Dancing.

28   **Squared Away**

Materials

individual photographs of the children   copy machine
laminating film   scissors or paper cutter

Activity

Enlarge the photographs on a copy machine. Trim each copy to make a square. Laminate the squares, then cut them into four or eight equal squares to make puzzles. Have the children put their puzzles together and describe both the pieces and the finished puzzle.

29   Folding Squares

Materials

square plastic tablecloth or blanket
square sheet of construction paper for each child

Activity

Demonstrate folding the tablecloth in half. Ask the children to identify the shape you've formed. Have the children fold their paper to match it. Fold the tablecloth again to make a square. Ask the children to identify the new shape. Let the children fold their paper to match. Help children understand that the only difference between squares and rectangles is the proportions (lengths) of their sides.

30   Bag Blocks

Materials

paper grocery sacks
newspaper
empty paper towel tube
duct tape

Activity

Invite the children to help fill the sacks about half full with wadded-up newspaper. Use the paper towel tube to measure the height of the fill-line (it should equal the length of the bottom of the bag). Fold down the tops of the sacks and tape them shut. Invite the children to use the square bag blocks for building.

31   Stack-a-Square

Materials

empty square pizza boxes (preferably small ones)
construction paper

Activity

Cut a strip of construction paper the length of one side of a pizza box. Invite the children to stack the boxes until their height equals the length of the construction paper strip. Ask the children to describe what they've just built. Tape the stacked boxes together to make a cube. Encourage the children to measure every side with the construction paper strip. Is every side the same?

 GENERAL ACTIVITIES

ACTIVITIES **32** TO **40**

32   Roll a Shape

Materials

square, circle, oval, rectangle and triangle shapes cut from poster board

Activity

Encourage the children to find out which shapes will roll and which won't.

33   Shape Hunt

Materials

square, circle, oval, rectangle and triangle shapes cut from construction paper

Activity

Divide the class into five teams and give each team one of the shapes. Send the teams on a hunt around the room for items that match the shape they were assigned. Suggest that each team use tally marks on their cut-out shape to record their findings.

34 Geoboards

Materials
geoboards
rubber bands

Activity
Encourage children to explore making shapes with the rubber bands on the geoboards.

35 Flannel Board Shapes

Materials
felt pieces cut in circles, ovals, squares, rectangles and triangles

Activity
Demonstrate making pictures by combining the various shapes and then leave children to their own creations.

36 Concentration Shapes

Materials
ten index cards with shapes drawn on them—two squares, two circles, two ovals, two rectangles, two triangles

Activity
Encourage the children to turn the cards face down and play Concentration.

37   Jiggly Shapes

Materials

gelatin mix
water
shallow pan
shape cookie cutters
spatula

Activity

Prepare gelatin mix, using about half the water directions call for. Pour into a shallow pan and refrigerate. When the gelatin is set, invite children to cut it into shapes using the cookie cutters. To remove the shapes, dip the bottom of the pan in warm water. Slide the spatula under the shapes and lift out. Let children eat their gelatin shapes.

38   Floor Puzzles

Materials

five sheets of poster board (different colors, if available)
scissors

Activity

Cut five large shapes—circle, oval, rectangle, square and triangle—out of the poster board. Cut each shape into two to four pieces (depending on the age and abilities of the children) to make big shape puzzles. Encourage children to put the puzzles together.

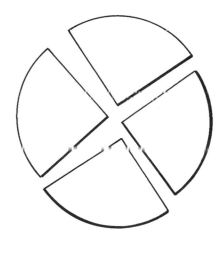

39   Gadget Printing

Materials

kitchen gadgets (potato masher, plastic cup, meat pounder, grater, funnel, etc.)
tempera paints
paper

Activity

Invite the children to dip the gadgets in the paint and make prints on their paper. Encourage them to identify the shapes they see in their prints.

40   Mystery Shapes

Materials

square block
rectangular block
triangular block
plastic egg
small ball
feely bag
index cards with the five shapes drawn on them

Activity

Place the index cards face down on a table. Put the other objects inside the bag. Invite children to draw a card, then reach into the bag and, without looking, find the matching shape.

Any Time Ideas

◆ Look for shapes outside the classroom when you go on field trips, to the library or to another classroom.
◆ Pay attention to food and containers at lunch time and snack time. Many times they represent a shape.

Suggestions for Home Involvement

◆ Encourage children to bring a toy from home that represents one of the shapes, or each shape when it is introduced. Ask the children to describe their toys during sharing time.
◆ Send home a copy of Home Connections on page 204.

Observations and Evaluations

◆ Describe each shape and ask the children to identify it.
◆ Show the children each shape and ask them to identify and describe it.

Resources

Children's Books

Carle, Eric. *My Very First Book of Shapes*. HarperCollins, 1985.
Ehlert, Lois. *Color Zoo*. HarperCollins, 1989.
Grifalconi, Ann. *The Village of Round and Square Houses*. Little Brown, 1986.
Hoban, Tana. *Shapes, Shapes, Shapes*. Greenwillow, 1986.
___. *Circles, Triangles, and Squares*. Greenwillow, 1974.
___. *Round and Round and Round*. Greenwillow, 1983.
Reiss, John. *Shapes*. Simon & Schuster, 1982.
Rogers, Paul. *The Shapes Game*. Holt, 1990.

Records and Songs

Millang, Steve and Greg Scelsa. "Round In a Circle." *We All Live Together, Volume 1*. Youngheart.
___. "Shapes." *We All Live Together, Volume 3*. Youngheart.

Home Connections

What's New?   Shapes!

We are learning about shapes—circles, ovals, squares, rectangles and triangles. Soon we will know that each shape has a specific number of sides and corners. We are discovering, for example, that the length (or "longness") and height (or "shortness") of sides can mean the difference between a rectangle and a square. Children's ability to identify shapes lays a foundation for understanding the principles of geometry.

Fun and Easy Things You Can Do at Home

◆ Encourage your child to look for road signs and name their shapes.
◆ Buy shaped crackers to share for a snack. Sort them according to shape before you eat them.
◆ Go for a walk and look for shapes in things. What shape is a window? A door? A roof? A section of sidewalk? A building? A van? A wheel?

Vocabulary Builders

These are some of our vocabulary words. Use them at home whenever you can.

circle	corner
oval	rectangle
side	square
triangle	

Book Corner

Next time you visit the library, check out one of these books:
Carle, Eric. *My Very First Book of Shapes.* HarperCollins, 1985.
Grifalconi, Ann. *The Village of Round and Square Houses.* Little Brown, 1986.
Hoban, Tana. *Circles, Triangles, and Squares.* Greenwillow, 1974.

This page may be copied and sent home to parents.

Count on Math

Chapter 9
Numeration 6 – 10

Definition

Numeration is discovering and understanding the "manyness" of numbers. In this chapter, children will develop an understanding of the "manyness" of the numbers six through ten. They will explore number families, learn to recognize numerals for each number, and practice simple operations. Understanding that a set remains the same no matter what its configuration is an important part of children's conceptual understanding of number value. Addition is the union of sets. Subtraction is the inverse of addition, or the taking apart of sets.

Bridge to Other Math Concepts

When children can recognize sets of objects with five or fewer members, they are ready to begin working on numbers six through nine. They will need to utilize the skill of "counting on." When they are called upon to count a set of eight flowers, they can do it without starting at one because they can mentally note a group of four and then count on: five, six, seven, eight. In this chapter children will develop and practice the skill of counting on.

Suggestions for Success

◆ Before beginning this chapter, repeat Activities 13 and 14 in Chapter 7. Encourage children to practice holding images of one to five objects in their heads. This is the foundation for counting on.
◆ Complete Activities 2 through 18 in this chapter with the number six, then repeat them for seven, eight, nine and ten.
◆ Remember to introduce each new number as adding one to the previously studied set.

Key Words

adding on	addition	counting on
eight	empty set	member
nine	number	number family
numeral	set	seven
six	subtraction	symbol
zero	ten	

1

Circle Time Story:
Mrs. Granger's Flower Bed

Materials

eight plastic flowers

Mike and Sarah were on their way to the bus stop. They walked the same path every morning: out the gate in their front yard, past the old oak tree on the corner, across the street and past Mrs. Granger's house to the bus stop.

It was a bright, sunny May day. The children couldn't help but notice all the beautiful flowers that were in bloom everywhere.

"Look," said Sarah, "Mrs. Granger has five flowers in her flower bed."

"Wow!" said Mike. "How did you count those so fast?"

"It's easy. I can see two red flowers and three yellow flowers. Two and three make five."

"I'll be glad when I can count like that," said Mike.

Several days later, Mike and Sarah walked out the gate in their front yard, past the old oak tree at the corner, across the street and past Mrs. Granger's house to the bus stop.

"Oh, my!" said Sarah. "Look! Mrs. Granger has eight flowers. Five from the other day and six, seven and eight by the fence."

"I want to count like that!" said Mike.

"It's easy. It's called counting on. You can always see five things and know it's five at a glance. Then you don't have to start with one. It saves time."

"You're smart, Sarah. When I'm in kindergarten, I'll be smart, too."

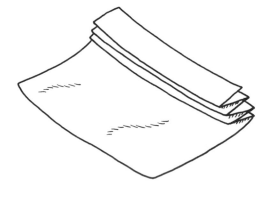

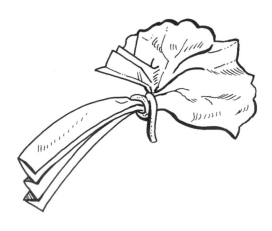

Materials for Story Extension

tissue paper
pipe cleaners

Activity

Encourage children to fold a sheet of tissue paper accordion-style and wrap a pipe cleaner around the middle. Show children how to pull the edges of the tissue paper up to make a big flower.

 2

Children Combinations

Materials

masking tape, rope or yarn

Activity

Place a strip of masking tape, rope or yarn on the floor. Ask six children to stand on one side of the tape. Ask the remaining children how many children are in the set. When they state that there are six children, move one of the children to the other side of the tape. Ask the children if the set is still six. Demonstrate all the set combinations for six.

 3

Number Bags

Materials

ziplock bags (one per child)
permanent marker
small counters (washers, pennies, buttons, etc.)

Activity

Put six counters inside each ziplock bag and seal it. Use a permanent marker to make a vertical line down the middle of the bag from the top (the "zippered" side) to the bottom. Show children how to move the counters on either side of the line to create set combinations. Allow enough practice for children to internalize the concept that six is six no matter what the combination or configuration of its members.

4   Drop a Set and Record

Materials

paper plate
washers (spray painted on one side)
drawing paper, two colors of construction paper squares
glue

Activity

Give the children six washers and encourage them to drop them onto a paper plate. Ask them to describe the set combination formed by the two colors of washers. Encourage the children to glue construction paper squares on a piece of drawing paper to represent the set combination.

5   Visual Sets

Materials

six counters or six pennies
paper
overhead projector

Activity

Place up to six pennies or counters on the overhead. Turn the overhead on and off quickly. Ask the children to identify the set they saw. Change the set and continue the activity.

6   Symbol

Materials

index card for each child
counters
ink pads

Activity

Draw the numeral 6 on the index cards and give them to the children. Ask the children to place six counters on their cards. Explain that the symbol on the card represents six. Let the children use the ink pad to make fingerprints around the numeral.

7   **Playdough Numerals**

Materials
playdough

Activity
Give the children playdough and encourage them to make the numeral 6.

 8   **Numeral Rubbings**

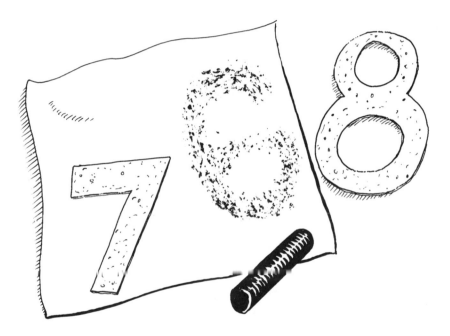

Materials
sandpaper
drawing paper
crayons

Activity
Cut numerals out of sandpaper and allow children to make crayon rubbings
of them.

9   Grainy Numerals

Materials

salt or sand
cookie sheet or shallow box

Activity

Fill a cookie sheet or shallow box with sand or salt and have the children draw numerals with their fingers.

10   Numeral Hunt

Material

Activity

Encourage children to go on a numeral hunt to find classroom items that have the numeral 6 on them (clock, calendar, book pages, games).

 COUNTING

ACTIVITIES **11** TO **16**

11   Number Plates

Materials

paper plates
buttons or other counters

Activity

Write one of the numerals 0-6 on each plate. Invite children to count the corresponding number of buttons or counters onto each plate.

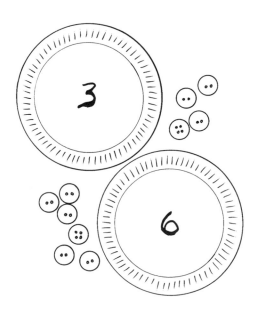

12

I Can Count

Materials
index cards
paper clips

Activity
Write one of the numerals 0-6 on each card. Encourage children to count the corresponding number of paper clips onto the numeral cards and then clip them to the cards.

 13

Bell Bags

Materials
4" x 8" piece of felt
1" strip of Velcro
six jingle bells
appliqué, numeral 6
bell bags from Activity 36 in Chapter 7

Activity
Fold the piece of felt in half and hot glue the sides to form a bag. Glue the numeral 6 on the outside of the bag. Glue the Velcro strip at the top to form a clasp. Put the six bells inside the bag. Invite children to explore the bag. Encourage them to order all the bell bags in different ways—numerical order, lightest to heaviest and softest sound to loudest sound. Does the arrangement change or stay the same?

 14

Number Book

Materials
number books from Activity 4 in Chapter 7
ziplock bags
pieces of poster board cut to fit inside the baggies

Activity
Let children add a page for six to their number books.

15   **Number Kites**

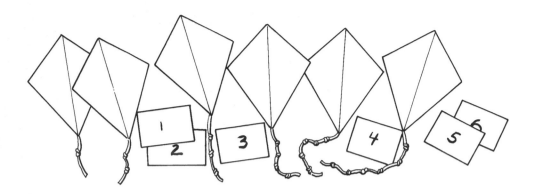

Materials

kites from Activity 40 in Chapter 6
index cards with numerals 1-6 written on them
materials for another kite (construction paper, rope)

Activity

Encourage children to match numeral cards to kites according to the number of knots tied in the tail of each kite. Let the children make a kite of their own to represent the number six.

16   **Numbers on a Rope**

Materials

number line on a rope from Activity 29 in Chapter 7
construction paper
markers

Activity

Write the numeral 6 on a sheet of construction paper and laminate. Punch holes and add to the number line rope. Ask the children to take six steps on the number line and check to see if they are standing on the numeral 6.

17   Counting on Cubes

Materials

two small boxes or sponge
      cut into two cubes
marker

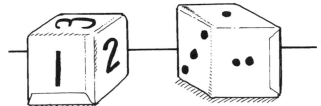

Activity

Make two number cubes
by covering small boxes
with contact paper or
cutting sponges into cubes.
Write numerals 1, 2 and 3
on three sides of one cube.
Put one to three dots on three sides of the other cube. Have children roll the
cubes. Ask them to name the numeral and then use the dots to count on and
determine the total number represented on the cubes.

Note: When you introduce the number seven, add the numeral 4 to the numeral
cube, but don't add four dots to the dot cube. (The total number possible will be
seven.) When you introduce the number eight, add four dots to the dot cube.
When you introduce the number nine, add the numeral 5 to the numeral cube or
add five dots to the dot cube.

18   Cards and Counters

Materials

the one of hearts through the six of hearts from a deck of playing cards
heart-shaped cutouts

Activity

Have the children draw a card and then count on using the heart cutouts to determine how many more hearts are needed to make six.

 **19**   # Number Cubes

Materials

two number cubes (see Activity 17) with the numerals 0-5 on each
strip of 2″ x 10″ paper divided into 2″ squares
crayons or markers

Activity

Have the children roll the number cubes and look at the numbers. Encourage them to use one color to color in the number of squares corresponding to the numeral on one cube. Use another color to color in the number of squares corresponding to the other cube. Encourage children to verbalize the number sentence they've illustrated.

 20   # Number Line Addition

Materials

number line on a rope (see Activity 29 in Chapter 7)
two number cubes with the numerals 0-5 on each (see Activity 19)

Activity

Lay the number line on the floor. Invite one child to stand on 0. Ask another child to roll the cubes. Have the child on the number line walk to the numeral showing on one cube. Ask the children to predict where the walker will end up after walking the additional steps showing on the other cube. Invite the child to take the additional steps and check the predictions.

Addition Sacks

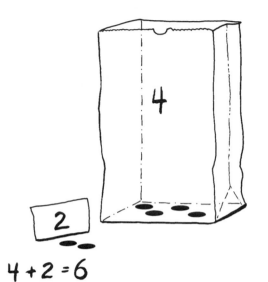

SACK NUMBER	NUMBER OF COUNTERS	NUMERAL CARDS
0	0	0, 1, 2, 3, 4, 5, 6, 7, 8, 9 10
1	1	0, 1, 2, 3, 4, 5, 6, 7, 8, 9
2	2	0, 1, 2, 3, 4, 5, 6, 7, 8
3	3	0, 1, 2, 3, 4, 5, 6, 7,
4	4	0, 1, 2, 3, 4, 5, 6
5	5	0, 1, 2, 3, 4, 5
6	6	0, 1, 2, 3, 4
7	7	0, 1, 2, 3
8	8	0, 1, 2
9	9	0, 1
10	10	0

$$4 + 2 = 6$$

Materials

eleven paper sacks   index cards
markers   counters

Activity

Write the numerals 0-10 on the sacks. Make numeral cards for each sack by writing the numerals shown in the chart on index cards. Stack each set of cards in front of the appropriate sack and place the number of counters shown on the chart inside the sack. Invite children to draw a card, add the number of counters shown on the card to those in the sack and state the total number of counters. The number of counters in the sack will validate their answer. Encourage children to say a number sentence that explains what they've done.

22   Mother, May I?

Materials

Activity

Invite the children to play "Mother, May I?" They may ask to take one to ten steps at each turn.

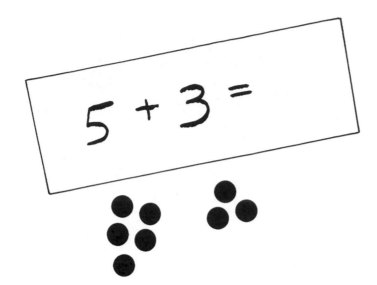

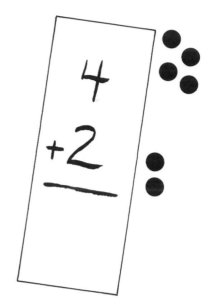

Materials

poster board
marker
counters

Activity

Write number sentences on strips of poster board. Invite children to use counters to figure out the answers. (Be sure to write sentences horizontally and vertically.)

24   # Ten in the Bed

Materials

butcher paper
recording of "Ten in the Bed," optional

Activity

Invite ten children to lie across the butcher paper and pretend to sleep. They should all face the same way. Play or sing "Ten in the Bed" and encourage the children to act it out. Depending on which version of the song you use, one child will be left to say "Goodnight" or all the children will eventually roll off, leaving zero.

25 Subtraction Sacks

Materials

eleven paper sacks   index cards
markers   counters

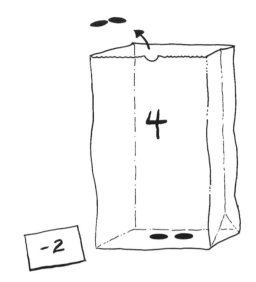

SACK NUMBER	NUMBER OF COUNTERS	NUMERAL CARDS
0	0	-0
1	1	-0, -1
2	2	-0, -1, -2
3	3	-0, -1, -2, -3
4	4	-0, -1, -2, -3, -4
5	5	-0, -1, -2, -3, -4, -5
6	6	-0, -1, -2, -3, -4, -5, -6
7	7	-0, -1, -2, -3, -4, -5, -6, -7
8	8	-0, -1, -2, -3, -4, -5, -6, -7, -8
9	9	-0, -1, -2, -3, -4, -5, -6, -7, -8, -9, -10
10	10	-0, -1, -2, -3, -4, -5, -6, -7, -8, -9, -10

$$4 - 2 = 2$$

Activity

Write the numerals 0-10 on the sacks. Make numeral cards for each sack by writing the numerals shown in the chart on index cards. Stack each set of cards in front of the appropriate sack and place the number of counters shown in the chart inside the sack. Invite children to draw a card, subtract the number of counters shown on the card from those in the sack and state the total number of counters. The number of counters in the sack will validate their answer. Encourage children to say a number sentence that explains what they've done.

26 Beanbag Drop

Materials

beanbags
box

Activity

Each child starts with ten beanbags. Encourage them to drop the beanbags into the box. Use the beanbags inside and outside the box to make up number sentences. For example, if five beanbags land outside the box and five land inside the box, say, "Ten minus five equals five," or "You started with ten beanbags, five are in the box. How many are left on the floor?"

27   Zip to Zero

Materials

ten counters for each child
one die

Activity

Encourage children to take turns rolling the die. Each time they roll, they subtract the number of counters shown on the die from their stack of ten. The first player to get rid of all the counters wins. Encourage children to create a number sentence after each turn to explain what they've done.

28   Drop a Hanky

Materials

counters
paper plate
facial tissue

Activity

Place up to ten counters on a paper plate, then invite a child to drop the tissue over them. Use the covered and uncovered counters to create number sentences. For example, you started with ten counters on the plate and the tissue covers four of them. Say, "Ten minus four equals six." You can also do this activity with an overhead projector. Use a sheet of paper to cover counters.

Any Time Ideas

◆ Show children the numerals on book pages (up to the numeral children are familiar with).
◆ When counting is appropriate, model its use. For example, taking attendance, making a lunch count, noting the number of children born in a specific month or lining up for a field trip.
◆ Perform fingerplays or sing songs that focus on numbers such as "Three Little Monkeys Jumping on the Bed," "This Old Man" and "Roll Over."

Suggestions for Home Involvement

◆ Ask children to bring a sheet of paper with their address and phone number on it to school. Discuss the real-life use of numbers in daily life.
◆ Send home a copy of Home Connections on page 220.

Observations and Evaluations

◆ Ask children to demonstrate set combinations for six, seven, eight, nine and ten.
◆ Ask children to identify the numerals 6, 7, 8, 9 and 10.
◆ Ask children to demonstrate counting the items in a set with six members. After they have counted, ask them to show you six. If they hand you the set, it indicates they have a conceptual understanding of six. If they hand you the item in the sixth position, repeat Activities 2-5. Do the same activity for numbers to ten.
◆ Ask children to demonstrate counting on by using the cubes in Activity 17.

Resources

Children's Books

Adams, Pam. *There Were Ten in the Bed*. Child's Play, 1979.
Bang, Molly. *Ten, Nine, Eight*. Greenwillow, 1983.
Coats, Laura J. *Ten Little Animals*. Simon & Schuster, 1990.
Crews, Donald. *Ten Black Dots*. Greenwillow, 1986.
Gerstein, Mordecai. *Roll Over!* Crown, 1988.
Grossman, Virginia, and Sylvia Long. *Ten Little Rabbits*. Chronicle, 1991.
Hague, Kathleen. *Numbears: A Counting Book*. Holt, 1986.
Linden, Ann Marie. *One Smiling Grandma: A Caribbean Counting Book*. Puffin, 1995.
Mahy, Margaret. *Seven Chinese Brothers*. Scholastic, 1990.
West, Colin. *One Little Elephant*. Children's Press, 1987.

Records and Songs

Beall, Pamela Conn and Susan Hagen Nipp. "This Old Man." *Wee Sing Nursery Rhymes and Lullabies*. Price Stern Sloan.
Raffi. "Six Little Ducks." *More Singable Songs*. A&M Records.
Scruggs, Joe. "Roll Over." *Deep in the Jungle*. Shadow Play.
Sharon, Lois and Bram. "One Elephant, Deux Elephants." *One Elephant, Deux Elephants*. Elephant.
"Roll Over." *Where Is Thumbkin?* Kimbo.

Home Connections

What's New?   Numeration 6-10!

We're working with the numbers six, seven, eight, nine and ten. Children are using the skills and understanding they gained while working with numbers one through five. They are exploring number families, learning to recognize numerals for each number and practicing simple addition and subtraction operations.

Fun and Easy Things You Can Do at Home

◆ Call attention to numerals on clocks, calendars, television channels, license plates, book pages and any other place you see them.
◆ Play games that require you to roll dice.
◆ Say counting rhymes such as "One, Two, Buckle My Shoe" and sing counting songs such as "This Old Man."

Vocabulary Builders

These are some of our vocabulary words. Use them at home whenever you can.

addition	counting on
equals	minus
number	plus
numeral	six/seven/eight/nine/ten
subtraction	

Book Corner

Next time you visit the library, check out one of these books:

Gerstein, Mordecai. *Roll Over!* Crown, 1988.

Hague, Kathleen. *Numbears: A Counting Book.* Holt, 1986.

Linden, Ann Marie. *One Smiling Grandma: A Caribbean Counting Book.* Puffin, 1995.

Mahy, Margaret. *Seven Chinese Brothers.* Scholastic, 1990.

This page may be copied and sent home to parents.

Chapter 10

Fractions

Definition

Fractions are parts of a whole. Learning about fractions teaches children the concept that things can be divided evenly. They also learn that their one-fourth of a cookie is the same amount as their friend's one-fourth of a cookie, the concept that the same fractional parts are equivalent parts of a whole.

Bridge to Other Math Concepts

Children need to understand whole numbers before they can understand that numbers can be expressed as part of a whole. Generally, young children intuitively understand parts. They may say, "Your half is bigger," even though they are unaware how to prove or disprove their conclusion. Children need to understand parts of numbers in order to understand measurement, time and money, which can all be expressed as equivalent parts of a whole (1/4 of a foot, a quarter after 7:00, one-half dollar, etc.).

Suggestions for Success

◆ Continue to remind children that fractions help us divide things evenly and fairly.
◆ Model correct language as you work with children. If you ask a child, "Give half the playdough to your friend," say, "We have one ball of playdough that we are going to divide into two equal parts."
◆ Children will need a lot of practice determining fractional parts. It is easier for them to see solids divided evenly than it is for them to see sets of objects divided evenly.

Key Words

divide	denominator
equal	fourth
fraction	half
numerator	part
share	third
whole	

Circle Time Story:
Learning to Share

Materials

twelve or twenty-four blocks

Mike and Steve were best friends. They did everything together. They liked all the same things. They were inseparable.

When they made a sandwich, they would cut it in half because they both liked peanut butter. When they slept out in the tent in the back yard, they could divide the space in half because they each needed the same amount of space.

When the boys built forts with Mike's blocks, they would each take half the blocks because they were going to build the same fort anyway. They had the perfect arrangement. Everything was great, until Tiffany moved in next door.

Now half didn't work anymore. Nothing worked. Tiffany liked all the same things but half left no sandwich for Tiffany, no space in the tent and no blocks.

One day Mike's mother heard the children fussing over the blocks. "Children," she said, "There is an easy solution. We can divide the blocks fairly among all of you."

She sat the children down and began to pass the blocks out one at a time. One to Mike, one to Steve and one to Tiffany. She went around again and again until all the blocks had been passed out. "Now we have divided the blocks into thirds, one third to each of you." she said. "You can do the same with your sandwich and with the space in the tent."

Everything was great again . . . that is, until Richele came over to play with Tiffany.

"Okay," said Steve, after the children began arguing over the blocks again. "Let's try what your mom taught us, Mike. We have one set of blocks and four kids. Let's divide the blocks into fourths."

The children sat down in a circle and each took a block out of the block bin. They did this again and again until all the blocks were gone. "Wow!" said Mike, "this really works!"

And all the children were happy. They shared everything—sandwiches, tent space, candy bars, blocks, crayons and pizzas. When Mike and Steve played, two children each had half. When Tiffany came over, three children each had one third. And when Richele was there, four children each had one fourth.

Count on Math

Materials for Story Extension

Activity

Select two boys to come to the front of the room to be Mike and Steve. Ask the children how many pieces they would have to cut a sandwich into for Mike and Steve? After the children answer two, add a girl to the group to represent Tiffany. Ask the children how many children and how many pieces of sandwich again. Continue by adding another child to represent Richele and repeat the question. This activity should help reinforce the concept of equal parts: two children—two equal parts, three children—three equal parts, four children—four equal parts.

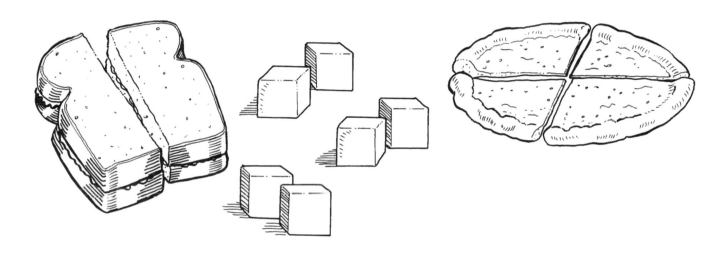

2   **Fractional Snacks**

Materials

graham crackers

Activity

Divide the children into groups of four. Give each group a whole (four sections) graham cracker. Ask the children to determine how they can divide the cracker fairly just like the children in the story had to divide their sandwich fairly. After children break the crackers into fourths, ask them to check to be sure all the parts are equal. Let the children eat their cookies. Try the activity again with children in groups of two.

Lines of Symmetry

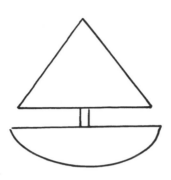

Materials

paper cutouts of several different shapes (apples, hearts, flowers, sailboats, trees—some of the shapes should be symmetrical and some should not)
scissors

Activity

Give pairs of children several of the cutouts. Ask them whether or not they think their cutouts can be divided fairly. Have the children fold the cutouts in half and check to see if the edges are even. If the edges are even, then the cutout can be divided fairly. Provide scissors so that children can unfold the cutouts and cut along the line of symmetry to create halves. Some of the cutouts will not be symmetrical. Discuss with the children that some of the cutouts cannot be cut into halves because they cannot be folded evenly.

 4

Sharing Playdough

Materials

playdough

Activity

Provide a large ball of playdough for a group of four children. Encourage children to think of ways they can share the playdough fairly. Model the appropriate language, "We have one ball of playdough and we need to divide it into four equal parts." You might want to let each child have a turn dividing the playdough, making sure the other three children choose their pieces first.

5   # Can Everything Be Shared?

Materials

four socks
four rocks
four hammers
four flat pieces of wood
chart paper, marker

Activity

Ask children if they think they will always be able to divide things fairly. Write their predictions on chart paper. Divide the class into four groups. Give each group a rock, a sock, a hammer and a piece of wood. Instruct each group to place the rock in the sock, place the sock on top of the wood and use the hammer to break the rock into equal parts for everyone in the group. What happens? Have the children generate a list of items that they could not divide equally (block, book, paintbrush, etc.).

Caution: Use this activity with children who are old enough to handle the hammer properly. Supervise closely.

 6   # Halves and Fourths

Materials

two 4″ squares of construction paper for each child
one piece of drawing paper for each child
scissors
glue

Activity

Have children fold one piece of their construction paper in half. Cut the square on the fold line. Identify each piece as half. Encourage the children to glue the two halves onto their drawing paper. Now have the children fold their remaining piece of construction paper in half, then in half again. Cut the square on the fold lines. Identify each piece as one fourth. Encourage the children to glue the one-fourth pieces on their drawing paper.

7   Floor Puzzles

Materials

poster board
scissors

Activity

Cut pieces of poster board into equal parts (halves, fourths, thirds, etc.). Encourage the children to put the fraction puzzles together.

8   Symbols

Materials

construction paper representations of halves and fourths from Activity 6
index cards with different fractions written on them
crayons

Activity

Review Activity 6 and remind children that they cut one piece of paper into two pieces to create halves. Write the numeral 2 and explain that when we write a symbol for a fraction, the number on the bottom is called the denominator and it tells us how many pieces something is divided into. Write a 1 above the 2 and explain that the top number, called the numerator, tells how many of the pieces we have. Play a game with the children by showing them the fraction cards and asking them to tell you how many pieces something has been divided into and how many pieces they have.

9   Which One Is Bigger?

Materials

construction paper
scissors

Activity

Remind children of activities where they divided something into fractional parts.
Ask them which they think is bigger, one-half or one-fourth. After the children
have made their predictions, cut paper apart to show the pieces and decide
whether the children's predictions were right. Repeat the activity using one-third,
one-fifth and so on.

10   Part to Whole

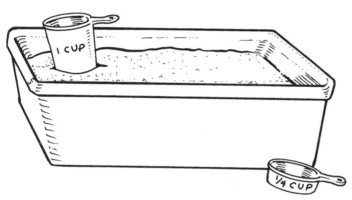

Materials

sand or water table
graduated measuring cups

Activity

Encourage children to explore and determine how
many of the 1/4 cups of water or sand it takes to fill
one cup. Continue exploring other fractional relationships. Repeat this type of activity frequently. Children
will need a lot of practice in order to internalize this
concept.

11   Name the Part

Materials

ice trays, egg cartons, candy boxes, other containers that are divided into sections

Activity

Encourage children to examine containers and tell the fraction that would represent one section of each. For example, one section of an ice tray equals one-
twelfth of the tray, one section of an egg carton equals one-twelfth, one section
of this candy box is one-tenth of the candy box.

Class Fractions

Materials

four sheets of paper or four carpet squares
blocks (enough that they can be evenly distributed among the children)

Activity

Place two pieces of paper or two carpet squares several feet apart on the floor in an open space. Tell the children you are going to divide the class into two equal parts. Go around the circle assigning every other child to one of the sheets of paper. If the number of children is uneven, join one of the groups. Now ask the children how they can create three equal groups. When the children determine that a new station should be added, do so and divide the class again. Repeat the activity, dividing the class into four equal groups. When you've formed four groups, give each group a bucket of blocks and have the children determine a way to divide the blocks evenly among all the members of their group.

Any Time Ideas

◆ Anytime snack or lunch items lend themselves to fractional parts, explore the possibilities with the children.
◆ When the class is divided for special activities, call attention to fractional parts.
◆ When the need for sharing materials arises in the classroom, let children help determine the solution.

Suggestions for Home Involvement

◆ Have children ask their parents to help them figure out which fractional part of their family they are. For example, if there are four people in a child's family, the child is one-fourth of the family.
◆ Send home a copy of Home Connections on page 230.

Observations and Evaluations

◆ Show children two cutouts—one that can be divided evenly, such as a heart, and one that can't, such as a sailboat. Ask the children to identify the cutout that can be divided evenly.
◆ Give children a piece of construction paper folded in half and a piece folded into fourths. Ask them to identify each.

Resources

Children's Books

Asch, Frank. *Moonbear*. Simon & Schuster, 1993.

Dragonwagon, Crescent. *Half a Moon and One Whole Star*. Simon & Schuster, 1986.

Hutchins, Pat. *The Doorbell Rang*. Greenwillow, 1986.

McMillan, Bruce. *Eating Fractions*. Scholastic, 1991.

Records and Songs

◆ "Ten in the Bed" Change the words to "Four in the Bed." Ask four children to lie on a piece of butcher paper on the floor. Talk about the fractional portion of the butcher paper bed that each child has. How do the portions change as each child rolls out?

◆ "I Have Sixpence" Put out six pennies in sets of two. Ask the children what fractional portion of the money each person mentioned in the song has. How does the portion change as the amount of money at the beginning of each verse changes?

Home Connections

What's New?   Fractions!

We are learning that things can be divided evenly and fairly and that numbers can be expressed as part of a whole. Children need to understand whole/part relationships in order to understand measurement, time and money, which we talk about in terms of parts of a whole (1/4 of a foot, a quarter after 7:00 and one-half dollar).

Fun and Easy Things You Can Do at Home

- ◆ Encourage your child to cut sandwiches into halves, quarters and thirds.
- ◆ Invite your child to help you in the kitchen, especially when you are measuring. Talk about cups, 1/2 cup, 1/4 teaspoon and so on.
- ◆ Give your child a plate of cookies and encourage him or her to divide them equally among friends.

Vocabulary Builders

These are some of our vocabulary words. Use them at home whenever you can.

divide	equal
fourth	fraction
half	part
share	whole

Book Corner

Next time you visit the library, check out one of these books:

Asch, Frank. *Moonbear.* Simon & Schuster, 1993.
Dragonwagon, Crescent. *Half a Moon and One Whole Star.* Macmillan, 1986.
Hutchins, Pat. *The Doorbell Rang.* Greenwillow, 1986.
McMillan, Bruce. *Eating Fractions.* Scholastic, 1991.

This page may be copied and sent home to parents.

Chapter 11

Measurement

Definition

Children learn how to measure by using a standard unit to describe and compare attributes (length, height, etc.) of objects. In this chapter, children will explore length, height, weight and capacity.

Bridge to Other Math Concepts

Children will need their understanding of part/whole relationships, comparing, ordering and numbers in order to develop an understanding of the use of measurement. Children will use measurement every time they encounter continuous materials. Because both time and money have standard units of measurement, children's understanding of measurement is essential to their ability to understand time and money.

Suggestions for Success

◆ Provide a variety of activities in which children have an opportunity to compare objects. This is the foundation of measurement.
◆ Allow children to begin measurement with non-standard or arbitrary units of measure (paper clip, handprint, etc.).
◆ Use as many real-life applications of measurement as you can in this chapter. The real world is filled with opportunities, and these real-life applications are a strong motivator for children.
◆ Review vocabulary related to comparisons in Chapter 6.

Key Words

big	centimeter
decimeter	foot
heavy	inch
light	measure
meter	ounce
pound	short
small	tall

Circle Time Story:
The July 4th Parade

Materials

red, white and blue streamers cut in several lengths—four inches to four feet

The children in Mrs. Pollard's classroom were filled with excitement. They were going to be in the Fourth of July Parade. Mrs. Pollard had told them to cut crepe paper streamers to carry in the parade, and each child was waiting patiently for a turn to choose a color and cut a streamer. Mrs. Pollard had told them they would practice their march during circle time.

When circle time finally arrived, the children sat with their streamers in their laps. Mrs. Pollard put on the music and asked the children to stand and march. And so they did.

"Oh my," said Mrs. Pollard, "Look at your streamers." Some were very short and others were very long. "I should have been more specific when I said to cut your own streamers. Our streamers should all be the same length. How can we do this?"

"I know," said Rebecca. "Let's choose the one that's the best length and use it to measure one for each of us."

"That's a great idea," said Mrs. Pollard.

And that's just what they did!

Materials for Story Extension

crepe paper streamers
scissors
marching music

Activity

Cut one piece of streamer 3' in length for children to use as a measure. Invite children to cut a streamer using yours as a model. When each child has a streamer, put on marching music and let the children march around the room waving their streamers.

2 Classroom Measurement

Materials

Activity

Ask the children to hold hands and form a line across the classroom. How many children wide is the classroom? Invite several children to walk toe-to-heel across the classroom as you count the number of their shoe lengths wide the classroom is. You should try the activity as well. Check answers. Are they the same?

3 Toe-to-Heel Measurement Again

Material

masking tape

Activity

Place a strip of masking tape on the floor. Have children walk toe-to-heel and count the number of steps it takes to walk the whole strip. Compare answers. Why do answers vary? How could everyone get the same answer? Help children arrive at the solution of needing a standard unit of measurement.

4 Teacher's Foot

Materials

construction paper cutouts of your foot, one for each child
masking tape

Activity

Ask the children to measure the masking tape line again, using the cutout of your foot. Are the measurements the same? Why?

5　Paper Clip Measuring

Materials
paper clips

Activity
Have children use paper clips as a standard unit of measure by linking them together to create a measuring chain. Encourage children to determine the height, length and width of several objects in the classroom. Compare answers and see if children came up with approximately the same measurement.

6　How Many Blocks?

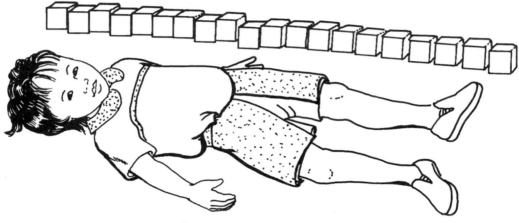

Materials
classroom blocks
bulletin board paper
chart paper for making a graph

Activities
Ask children to work in pairs. Have them take turns lying on the floor and measuring their heights by placing a row of blocks beside them. Record the height of each child in terms of how many blocks tall they are. When all children have been measured, make a class graph depicting how many blocks long each child is.

7   How Much Do I Weigh?

Materials

bathroom scales or doctor's scales
chart for graphing
a one pound bag of sugar or flour or any
    other item that weighs one pound

Activities

Weigh the children and record their weights. Discuss the fact that their weights are expressed in pounds. Use the one-pound bag of flour to help the children understand the concept of a pound. Ask the children to tell you how many bags of flour they would weigh. Make a class graph showing the children's weight.

8   Coffee Can Fillings

Materials

three one-pound coffee cans
packing peanuts
sand
water

Activity

Fill one coffee can with water, one can with sand and one can with packing peanuts. Ask the children to arrange the cans in order from heaviest to lightest. The cans are all the same size, why are their weights different?

9   Balance Scale Weigh-in

Materials

balance scale
several classroom objects (crayons, book)
block

Activity

Have the children weigh each of the classroom objects against a classroom block. Record the results. How many items weighed more than the block? How many weighed less than the block?

CAPACITY MEASUREMENT

ACTIVITIES **10** TO **12**

10   Children in a Box

Materials

large cardboard box (washing machine or refrigerator size)
variety of smaller size boxes

Activity

See how many children can fit in the box. Explain that the box has a capacity of ___ children. Place the other boxes in the block center and let the children see how many blocks will fit inside each one.

11   How Many Does It Take?

Materials

several containers of varying sizes
water
birdseed
sand

Activity

Provide many opportunities for children to explore capacity by providing the above materials for exploration. Ask how many small containers of sand, water or birdseed it takes to fill the larger container.

Estimating Water Levels

Materials

one small clear container
water
one large clear container
rubber band

Activity

Fill the small container half full of water. Ask children to estimate where the water from the small container will be when it is poured into the larger container. Have them mark their prediction by placing a rubber band at the level they estimate. Encourage children to pour the water in and check their estimate.

Any Time Ideas

◆ Call attention to measurement opportunities inherent in normal classroom activities (when building towers in the block center or rolling playdough in the fine motor center).
◆ Keep a scale and measurement chart in the classroom throughout the year. Periodically weigh and measure the children and make comparisons.
◆ Help children think about the capacity of a container when they are storing manipulatives in buckets.
◆ If children are allowed to pour their own juice at snack time, they will quickly learn about the capacity of the cup.

Suggestions for Home Involvement

◆ Have children find out from their parents how much they weighed at birth. Let them post this information beside the current information on the weight graph you did in class.

◆ Encourage children to bring a piece of yarn from home that is the same length as they were when they were born.

◆ Send home a copy of the Home Connections on page 239.

Observations and Evaluations

◆ Give the children a standard unit of measurement and ask them to measure the length of a table. If children cannot accomplish this, repeat Activities 2-6.

◆ Provide two objects. Ask children to use a balance scale to determine which object is heavier. If children cannot accomplish this, repeat Activities 7-9.

◆ Give the children sand, a jar and a scoop. Ask children to determine how many scoops of sand it will take to fill the jar. If children cannot accomplish this, repeat Activities 10-12.

Resources

Children's Books

Adams, Pam. *Ten Beads Tall.* Child's Play, 1989.
Allen, Pamela. *Who Sank the Boat?* Putnam, 1990.
Carle, Eric. *The Very Hungry Caterpillar.* Putnam, 1994.
Leedy, Loreen. *Big, Small, Short, Tall.* Holiday, 1987.
Lionni, Leo. *Inch by Inch.* Morrow, 1995.
Pluckrose, Henry. *Capacity.* Franklin Watts, 1995.
Ziefert, Harriet. *How Big Is Big?* Puffin, 1995.

Records and Songs

Sharon, Lois and Bram. "I'm Not Small." *One Elephant, Deux Elephants.* Elephant. "One Elephant." *Where Is Thumbkin?* Kimbo.

Home Connections

What's New?   Measurement!

We are exploring length, height, weight and capacity. We are learning about units of measurement like inches, feet, ounces and pounds. We are learning to use measuring cups and spoons, rulers and scales. Children will use measurement in many of their everyday experiences.

Fun and Easy Things You Can Do at Home

◆ Record your child's growth on a wall chart.
◆ Talk about things that are tall, short, long, heavy, light, small, big and so on.
◆ Give your child a ruler or tape measure and encourage him or her to measure furniture, rooms, crayons and other things in and around your home.

Vocabulary Builders

These are some of our vocabulary words. Use them at home whenever you can.

big	foot
heavy	inch
light	measure
ounce	pound
tall	short
small	

Book Corner

Next time you visit the library, check out one of these books:
Adams, Pam. *Ten Beads Tall*. Child's Play, 1989.
Carle, Eric. *The Very Hungry Caterpillar*. Putnam, 1994.
Leedy, Loreen. *Big, Small, Short, Tall*. Holiday, 1987.
Lionni, Leo. *Inch by Inch*. Morrow, 1995.

This page may be copied and sent home to parents.

Chapter 12

Time and Money

Definitions

Time is a unit of measurement. Money is a medium of exchange. In this chapter, children will be introduced to terms and concepts related to time and money, and they will begin using what they learn to build a foundation for later understanding.

Bridge to Other Math Concepts

Both time and money require an ability to conserve (recognize that an object does not change just because its configuration changes) and a firm grasp of measurement and fractions. Time and money are abstract and challenging concepts for young children. Both concepts will develop over time. This chapter is intended to be an introduction. Children will apply what they have learned about numbers, measurement and fractions to beginning time and money concepts.

Suggestions for Success

◆ Before teaching this chapter, assess the developmental maturity of your class. Time and money are abstract concepts and many children are not ready for these concepts until they are older. It is acceptable to wait to introduce these concepts.

◆ Begin with global concepts and work toward more specific concepts. For example, children can understand yesterday, today and tomorrow more easily than they can understand hours and minutes. Children can understand that money is used as an exchange for goods and services before they can equate a quarter with twenty-five pennies.

Key Words

TIME

afternoon	day	hour
minute	month	morning
night	seasons	time
today	tomorrow	week
year	yesterday	

MONEY

bill	coin	dime
nickel	penny	quarter

1

Circle Time Story: Waiting for School

Materials

Amber and Fonda were so excited that it was almost time for school to start. Every day they would ask their mother, "Is today the day?" Every day their mother would say, "No, not today." Then she would tell the girls how many more days they had to wait. Today she said, "There are nine more days until school starts."

One day the girls' grandmother heard them question their mother about how much longer until school started. She had an idea.

Amber and Fonda's grandmother took the calendar from the wall and her markers from the drawer and called the girls to come sit by her. She showed them the day on the calendar and let Amber put a big X on it. Then she showed them the date on the calendar when school would start. She let Amber make a big red circle around that date.

"Now," she said, "every morning when you wake up, you can mark a day off the calendar. When the last day is marked off, you'll know the next day is the first day of school."

Amber and Fonda were so excited. They had a way to keep up with the days! Their mother was excited, too.

Materials for Story Extension

calendar	hour glass
watch	clock
timer	stop watch

Activity

Show the children the tools used for measuring or tracking time. Describe each item and give examples of how people use it. Demonstrate any items that you can. For example, set a timer for two minutes and march for that length of time, or play a game or work a puzzle using the stop watch to measure the time each player spends on a turn. Use the classroom calendar to help children understand the concept of yesterday, today and tomorrow. The calendar also presents a good opportunity to introduce days of the week, months and seasons. Use a cutout or marker on the calendar to indicate a new day.

 2

Pictorial Record

Materials

chart paper or large sheet of butcher paper
crayons

Activity

Let the children dictate a list of things that take place in the morning. Ask them to do the same for things that take place in the afternoon and in the evening. Write a big numeral 1 and the word morning on the top of the paper. List a couple of the children's morning suggestions. Leave a space for the children to add illustrations. In the middle of the paper, write a large numeral 2 and the word afternoon. List a couple of the children's suggestions for afternoon activities. Leave a space for illustrations. On the bottom of the paper, write a large numeral 3 and the word evening. List a couple of the children's suggestions for evening activities there. Encourage the children to illustrate the activities for morning, afternoon and evening.

3 Sundial

Materials

6' stick
large rocks
clock

Activity

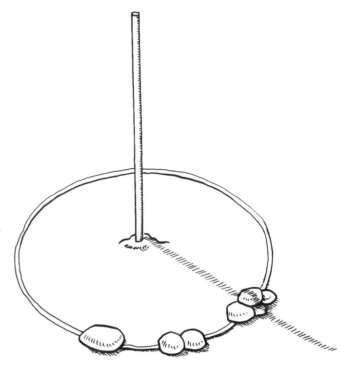

Make a sundial with the children. Find a sunny place outside. Push the stick in the dirt so that it stands up straight. Draw a circle around the stick. Use a big rock to mark the place on the circle where the shadow falls. Go outside and mark the new location of the shadow every couple of hours. Lead the children to understand that the shadow moves with the passing of time. Tell the children that people used sundials before watches and clocks were invented. Show the children a clock and call their attention to how the big hand moves around it just like the shadow moves around the circle.

4 Using the Clock

Materials

clock
colored stick-on dots

Activity

Use the stick-on dots to mark a few important events of the day on the clock. For example, you may want to mark snack time (9:00 am—red dots on 9 and 12), outdoor play (10:15 am—blue dots on 10 and 3), lunch (12:00—two green dots on 12), and time to go home (4:00 pm—yellow dots on 4 and 12). Mark one time, then add others when the children understand the concept. Show the children how to look at the hands of the clock when they begin these activities. Where are the hands in relation to the dots?

5   # Number Line Clock

Materials

rope number line (from Activity 16 in Chapter 9)
construction paper
marker

Activity

Add 11 and 12 to your rope number line. Have the children review walking the
number line. Form the number line into a circle. Lead children to understand that
the clock is basically a circular number line. Do several activities, inviting children to
step off hours on the clock. Don't worry about hands on the clock during this
activity.

 6   # A Clock of My Own

Materials

clean, empty margarine tub for each child
brass brads
plastic or cardboard
permanent markers
small strips of paper

Activity

Draw numbers for a clock face on the margarine tub lids. Cut large and small clock
hands from cardboard or plastic. Punch a hole through the end of each hand and
through the center of the margarine tub lids. Use the brad to attach the hands to
the lid. On small pieces of paper, write 1:00, 2:00, 3:00 and so on. Encourage children to draw a slip of paper and set their clock hands to show the time on the
paper. Children can store papers inside their tubs when not in use.

7

Circle Time Story:
Treasures in the Sandbox

Materials

Ryan was digging in his sandbox, making tunnels and hills and roads. As he lifted a pile of sand with his shovel, he noticed something shiny. He picked it up and put it in his bucket. He started to dig again, but he noticed another shiny object. Now he was intrigued. How many shiny objects are buried here? He began digging with a new purpose.

By the time Ryan was finished digging, he had found several shiny objects. Some of them looked alike and some were different from the others. He took his bucket in to his mother to show her his treasures.

Ryan's mother told him that he had found coins. She put the coins in stacks of those that looked alike. She told Ryan that the first stack was pennies, the second was nickels, the third was dimes and the last stack was quarters. "If you count all these coins," she said, "you will see that you have sixty-four cents."

Ryan took the money and put it in his bank. He was saving for a baseball bat and sixty-four cents would make a good contribution to his goal.

Materials for Story Extension

sand
pennies, nickels, dimes, quarters
strainers

Activity

Bury coins in the sand table or in a tub of sand. Let children dig with the strainers to find coins. Encourage the children to name the coins they find. It is likely you will have to provide some identification and vocabulary.

8   Sidewalk Art Show

Materials

announcement letter to families
children's artwork
donation box

Activity

Have children create several pieces of art for a sidewalk art show and sale. Send a letter to families announcing the sale. State that there will be no set prices, but each piece will be given away for a donation. The purpose of this activity is to establish the concept that money is an exchange for goods or services. On the day of the sale, line up the artworks outside and let family members make their selections and donations. Encourage children to be available to describe their art and to collect the donations. After the sale, count the money with the children and let them help you classify it into correct categories. This is a perfect opportunity to reinforce recognition and identification of coins and bills. Encourage the children to discuss what they would like to do with the money. They might want to donate it to a worthy cause, buy something for the classroom, or even save it for later. If they choose to buy something for the classroom, try to arrange a field trip and let them be involved in the purchase.

9   Grocery Store

Materials

clean, empty food boxes, vegetable cans, egg cartons, milk cartons, etc.
cash register
play money
signs

Activity

Invite the children to set up a grocery store and pretend they are buying and selling groceries. Don't worry about accuracy of payment for merchandise. The goal of this activity is simply to reinforce the concept that money serves as payment for goods.

10   Money Wheel

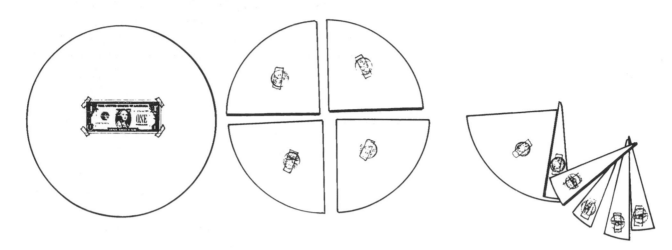

Materials

four large, round, cardboard pizza trays
four quarters
ten dimes
twenty nickels
a dollar bill
tape

Activity

Tape the dollar bill to the middle of one of the pizza trays. Cut the second pizza tray into fourths (four equal parts) and tape a quarter to each piece. Cut the third pizza tray in half, and then cut each half into fifths (five equal parts). Tape a dime to each of the ten pieces. Cut the last pizza tray into fourths and then cut each fourth into fifths (five equal parts). Tape a nickel to each of the twenty resulting pieces. Using the dollar board as a base, let the children manipulate the various pieces to determine how many of each coin it takes to equal a dollar or another coin. For example, they can place the four quarter pieces on top of the dollar tray to equal a dollar. Then if they want, they can stack five nickel pieces on top of one of the quarters and see a new arrangement. Or they can start by placing five dimes, one quarter and five nickels on top of the dollar tray to equal a dollar. Children will need lots of practice with this game, but will continue to internalize concepts as they manipulate the pieces.

11   Lemonade Stand

Materials

lemonade in a pitcher
paper cups
sign

Count on Math

Activity

Help the children set up a lemonade stand. It might be a good idea to set it up at the end of the day and encourage family members and friends to be the customers. Sell the lemonade for a nickel and encourage the children to count nickels and pennies in change. If parents are participating, ask them to use either correct change or a dime for their purchase. Plan on helping children to make change.

12 Money Magic

Materials

two baby food jars
several pennies, nickels,
   dimes and quarters

Activity

Fill one jar with pennies. Fill the other jar about 1/2 full with nickels, dimes and quarters. Ask children to tell you which jar has the most money in it. Encourage children to sort and count the money from each jar to check their answers.

Any Time Ideas

◆ Encourage children to sort and identify coins they bring to school for lunches, milk, books and other things.
◆ Invite children to tell about things they did yesterday and things they will do tomorrow.

Suggestions for Home Involvement

◆ Invite families to donate items for the grocery store and to participate in the sidewalk art show and lemonade stand.
◆ Send home a copy of Home Connections on page 251.

Observations and Evaluations

This chapter is intended to be an introduction to time and money. Since both concepts are abstract and challenging for young children, it is too early to assess children's conceptual understanding.

Resources

Children's Books

Blos, Joan. *A Seed, a Flower, a Minute, an Hour*. Simon & Schuster, 1992.
Carle, Eric. *The Very Hungry Caterpillar*. Putnam, 1994.
Hutchins, Pat. *Clocks and More Clocks*. Simon & Schuster, 1970.
Llewellyn, Claire. *My First Book of Time*. DK Publishing, Inc., 1992.
Pienkowski, Jan. *Time*. Little Simon, 1990.
Rockwell, Anne. *Bear Child's Book of Hours*. HarperCollins, 1987.
Silverstein, Shel. "Smart" in *Where the Sidewalk Ends*. HarperCollins and Row, 1974.
Smalls-Hector, Irene. *Irene and the Big, Fine Nickel*. Little, Brown & Co., 1991.
Tafuri, Nancy. *All Year Long*. Greenwillow, 1983.
Viorst, Judith. Alexander, *Who Used to Be Rich Last Sunday*. Simon & Schuster, 1978.
Williams, Vera B. *A Chair for My Mother*. Morrow, 1988.

Records and Songs

James, Dixie L. and Linda C. Becht. *The Singing Calendar*. Kimbo.
Millang, Steve and Greg Scelsa. "Days of the Week English and Spanish." *We All Live Together, Volume 4*. Youngheart.

Home Connections

What's New?   Time and Money!

We are learning about time and money. We are talking about yesterday, today and tomorrow, days of the week and routines. We are also learning to recognize and identify bills and different coins. Both time and money will have many real-life applications throughout your child's life.

Fun and Easy Things You Can Do at Home

◆ Talk about your daily routine. Ask questions such as, "What comes next? What comes before? What comes later?"
◆ Talk about things that happened yesterday, things that happened today, things that will happen tomorrow.
◆ Give your child a small allowance and a bank. Help count the money every few days or whenever your child adds or takes away money.
◆ Encourage your child to sort coins and bills.

Vocabulary Builders

These are some of our vocabulary words. Use them at home whenever you can.

day/night	hour/minute
morning/afternoon/evening	yesterday/today/tomorrow
dime	nickel
penny	quarter

Book Corner

Next time you visit the library, check out one of these books:
Blos, Joan. *A Seed, a Flower, a Minute, an Hour*. Simon & Schuster, 1992.
Carle, Eric. *The Very Hungry Caterpillar*. Putnam, 1994.
Smalls-Hector, Irene. *Irene and the Big, Fine Nickel*. Little, Brown & Co., 1991.
Williams, Vera B. *A Chair for My Mother*. Morrow, 1988.

This page may be copied and sent home to parents.

Note: Enlarge drawings as needed.

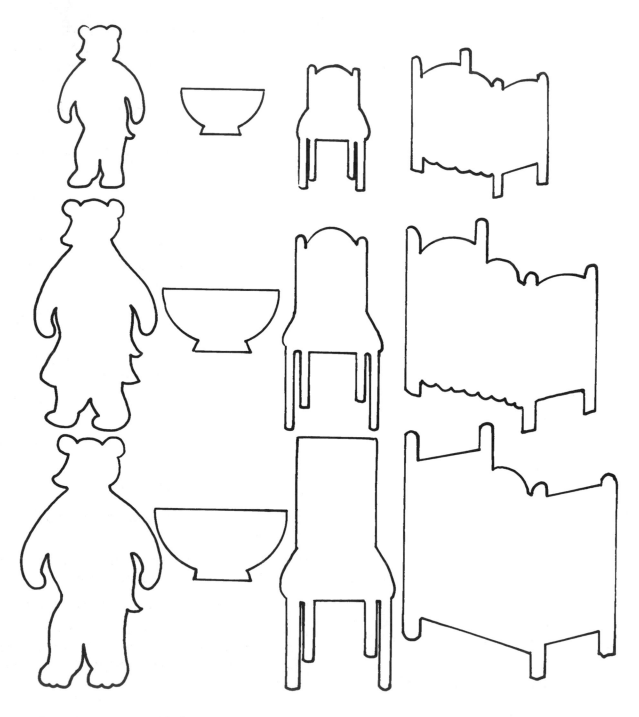

Note: Enlarge drawings as needed.

Glossary of Math Terminology

addition—the union of two (or more) sets

attributes—characteristics of an object such as color, shape, size

capacity—measure of the ability to receive, absorb or hold; volume

circle—a closed curve with all parts equally distant from the center point

classification—organization of objects based on likenesses and differences

comparisons—a statement of likenesses and differences

complex patterns—repetitive designs that utilize more than one attribute

concept—a general idea or understanding derived from specific instances or occurrences

conceptual understanding—the internalizing of information that connects skills and concepts

conservation—the ability to maintain an understanding of value or capacity of an item or set despite visual changes in that item or set

consistency in teaching—teaching in such a manner that instruction remains valid throughout the child's education

continuous materials—materials that can be measured (for example, water, sand, gravel)

counting—to name and assign value to items in a one-to-one order

counting on—to start with a specific known number and count from that point forward to determine the value of a set

descriptive language—language that identifies attributes of an object or set

developmental sequence—presenting skills and concepts in a sequence that allows children to take what they have learned and apply it to the next skill or concept

differences—ways in which items or objects are not alike

direction words—vocabulary that indicates the position of an item

discrete materials—materials that can be counted (for example, blocks, cookies, children)

fraction—a part of a whole

graph—mathematical tool used for organizing data and identifying patterns and trends

grouping—placing objects or items together based on a specific characteristic or attribute

hands-on, concrete experiences—opportunities for children to manipulate real objects

height—the distance from the base to the top of an object

length—the distance from the beginning to the end of an object

matching—to place like objects together

meaningful context—presenting material that fits into an existing scheme or plan

measurement—the dimension, capacity or quantity of something determined by a standard unit

money—currency, coins, issued by the government

non-standard unit of measure—use of non-traditional tools of measurement to determine the length, height or weight of an object (for example, blocks or paper clips)

number—a name assigned to a set of objects to determine how many members belong to that particular set (for example, three or five)

number value—how many objects are assigned to a given number

numeral—the written symbol representing the number of members of a set (for example, 3 or 5)

numeration—a system of numbers and number value

one-to-one correspondence—pairing or matching objects in a one-to-one relationship

order—the placement of sets or members of a set in an increasing or decreasing pattern

oval—a shape resembling an egg or ellipse; a closed curve with all parts not equally distant from the center point

pattern—a repetitive design

position words—vocabulary describing the location of an object

rectangle—a closed object with four corners and four right angles in which opposite sides are parallel and equal in length

sequence—an order of arrangement, one thing after another

set—a group of objects

set comparison—looking at the likenesses and differences of more than one group of objects

shapes—closed figures, something distinguished from its surrounding by its outline or form

similarities—the ways in which things are alike; likenesses

simple patterns—repetitive designs based on one attribute such as shape, color or size

spatial relationships—the manner in which objects are placed in relationship to another object

square—a closed figure with four corners, four right angles, with opposite sides parallel and all sides equal in length

standard unit of measure—customary unit used for determining the size, capacity or weight of an object (for example, cups or inches)

subtraction—the separation of part of a set from the whole or the difference in value of two sets

time—a unit of measure used to determine the duration of an event, such as minute, hour, day, week, month, year and so on

triangle—a three-sided closed figure with three corners and three interior angles

vocabulary development—developing an understanding for the meaning of words; learning the meaning of more words

weight—the heaviness of an object

width—the measurement of something from side to side

zero—name assigned to a set containing no members or the empty set

Index

Recommended Titles

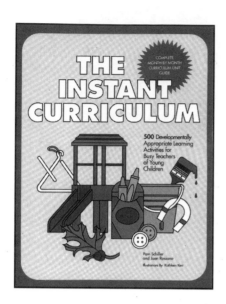

The Instant Curriculum
500 Developmentally Appropriate Learning Activities for Busy Teachers of Young Children

Pam Schiller and Joan Rossano

With very little planning and preparation you can do 500 different developmentally appropriate learning activities with children. You can use activities by month or by subject. A few of the subjects included in these ready-to-use activities are art, fine and gross motor skills, language, math, music, problem-solving, dramatic play and imagination, and critical thinking. It's easy to find the right activity for any day or purpose. 390 pages. © 1990.

ISBN 0-87659-124-1
Gryphon House
10014
Paperback

The Complete Learning Center Book
An Illustrated Guide to 32 Different Early Childhood Learning Centers

Rebecca Isbell

Enrich your classroom environment with unique learning centers and new ideas for traditional centers. All you ever needed to know about 32 learning centers is included in this comprehensive book. 365 pages. © 1995.

ISBN 0-87659-174-8
Gryphon House
17584
Paperback

Available at your favorite bookstore, school supply store or order from Gryphon House®

Where is Thumbkin?

500 Activities to Use with Songs You Already Know

Pam Schiller and Thomas Moore

These are the songs teachers and children are already singing together every day. The book is organized month-by-month, and has sections for toddlers, threes, fours, five and six year olds. These simple learning activities can be used in circle time, for transitions, or for special music time. A list of related children's literature and recordings accompanies each set of activities. 256 pages. © 1993.

ISBN 0-87659-164-0
Gryphon House
13156
Paperback

The Giant Encyclopedia of Circle Time and Group Activities for Children 3 to 6

Over 600 Favorite Activities Created by Teachers for Teachers

Edited by Kathy Charner

Filled with over 600 activities covering 48 themes, this book is jam-packed with ideas that were tested by teachers in the classroom. Many activities include suggestions on integrating the circle time or group activity into other areas of the curriculum. 510 pages. © 1996.

ISBN 0-87659-181-0
Gryphon House
16413
Paperback

***Available at your favorite bookstore,
school supply store or order from Gryphon House®***